Advance praise for Wesley

You Are Here

"This is an emotionally coplicated book of surface and
dep: it is hilarious and ppears to be a
bravura performce m. as you read on,
disdain deepens until it becomes despair, then deepens further
into compassion and finally love. *You Are Here* is dark and
sparkling, wonderfully intelligent, flip, and deeply felt."

— Mary Gaitskill,
author of *Bad Behavior*

"In *You Are Here,* Wesley Gibson brings his formidable nov-
elistic talents to the memoir/monologue. There is not a
wasted word here, no easy answers, no cheap comforts. He
has brought to his story of scratching out a living and trying
to find a home in New York City the consolation of humor —
the book *is* laugh-out-loud funny — and the even more sublime consolation of turning the whole tragic, harrowing mess
of it into art."

— Scott Spencer,
author of *A Ship Made of Paper*

"Wesley Gibson's contemporary New York memoir is vastly funny, compassionate, and entertaining. Written with breathtaking flourishes of wit and sensitivity, it gives an engaging picture of a young man winning the good fight to maintain his integrity in a hard and often ridiculous world."

— Edward Hower,
author of *A Garden of Demons*

"It is easy while reading this enthralling memoir to forget it isn't a novel. Gibson is that fine a storyteller and master of suspense. Here the lyrical is blended with the uproarious to superb effect. The reader finishes wanting only one thing: more Gibson."　　　　— Sigrid Nunez, author of *For Rouenna* and *Naked Sleeper*

"Wesley Gibson's memoir is incisive, strange, disquieting, and very funny. It is also beautifully written. Gibson possesses a glorious gift for metaphor: scarcely a page goes by without a verbal turn that surprises and delights. Anyone who has ever tried to find his or her bearings in a crazily skewed world will find much to celebrate here. I loved this book."

— Paul Russell, author of
The Coming Storm
and *War Against the Animals*

Also by Wesley Gibson

Shelter

You Are

• Here •

A Memoir of Arrival

Wesley Gibson

BACK BAY BOOKS
Little, Brown and Company
Boston · New York · London

First Edition

Author's note: The stories and characters in this book
are real, but the names Becky, Fred, Joe, and Mai are fictitious.

Library of Congress Cataloging-in-Publication Data
Gibson, Wesley.
    You are here : a memoir of arrival / by Wesley Gibson. — 1st ed.
        p.   cm.
    ISBN 0-316-74084-5
    1. Gibson, Wesley — Homes and haunts — New York (State) — New York.
2. New York (N.Y.) — Social life and customs — 20th century.   3. Novelists,
American — 20th century — Biography.   4. Young men — New York
(State) — New York.   I. Title.

PS3557 I2263Z478 2004
813'.54 — dc21
[B]   2003054551

10 9 8 7 6 5 4 3 2 1

Q-FF

Text design by Marie Mundaca

Printed in the United States of America

For my friends

You Are Here

That second day, I knew something was wrong. The apartment seemed, not quiet, but desolate. I was looking around, trying to feel at home. But it's hard to feel at home when you've moved in with a stranger named John, a man as pale and waxy and elongated as a candle, a man you met through a gay roommating service, a man who had seemed touchingly eager when he'd interviewed you, and you'd perched there on the edge of the love seat, giving the usual performance, trying to convey that you paid the bills on time but were also good for a few laughs, that you were a gourmet cook who liked nothing better than to whip up coquilles St. Jacques for yourself and whomever happened to be around, but that you wouldn't ever consider using his cream for your coquilles, that you were never there, at least not when he was, unless he wanted you to be, in which case you hoped you hadn't given the wrong impression, you actually were a homebody, someone who liked nothing better than to curl up around the VCR with a new friend and microwave popcorn, watching, what a coincidence, *Home for the Holidays* was your favorite movie too (note to self: find out what *Home for the Holidays* is).

I'd just moved back to New York. Studios were going for fifteen hundred. After first month's, last month's, a deposit, 10 percent for the agent, you were looking at five thousand dollars just to get in. That was my whole budget. That was if I was picked from the restless mob crowded around me with its own marked-up *Village Voice*s, in a room the size of a golf cart with a view of someone's filthy venetian blinds. People kid about New York; but they're not kidding.

John bit and invited me to rent a room in his apartment on the Upper East Side. It was larger than any studio I'd seen, and cheaper too, with a view of someone's garden. An elevator, a bathroom I shared with the other roommate — some guy named Alan, who actually was never there. A real live kitchen. Most of the kitchens I'd seen had been appliances shoved into closets. I'd marveled over this place to everyone I knew, and they'd listened with the polite disinterest of people who have apartments, before steering the conversation back to their more established lives.

But now the euphoria was wearing off, and the first thing I had noticed was that this place was not really my taste. I actually don't know what my taste is, or if I even have taste, but this was not it. This was suburban, but stitched through with New Age Kitsch. Who even knew there was New Age Kitsch? There was a plaid living-room suite, circa 19-hideous-something; but little wizards made from crystals formed tiny gesticulating groups on end tables, on top of the gigantic TV. They were arranged in a lit brass-and-glass sort of exhibition case. There were vases of bridesmaid's-dress-pink cloth flowers; but dreamcatchers were nailed to the wall. An answering machine blinking its red light with about sixty messages sat next to . . . Wait. An answering machine with sixty messages. It was probably nothing; maybe he just didn't erase. But something, the hazy August day (that was another thing, it turned out the central air-conditioning didn't work), the morguelike calm, the disconcerting juxtapositions — Southwestern prayer rugs hanging next to reproductions of enormous-eyed-children paintings . . . The day was a conspiracy, and my mind was weak from the dislocations of moving. John was a serial killer. Of course. Innocent boy from small city. Next thing you know you're nothing but a few hacked-off limbs and severed eyeballs charred beyond recognition in the incinerator conveniently located down the hall.

I called Jo Ann.

"Hello?" She sounded like what she was: mildly depressed, somnolently moving through her life under the suicide gray of the Ithaca skies.

"It's me." I probably sounded like what I was too — mildly panicked, flutteringly paranoid (business as usual, really) — because she was suddenly alert and saying, "What's wrong?"

"I think the guy I moved in with is a serial killer," I whispered, looking around for a blunt object to stun him with in case he had the seismographic hearing nine out of ten psychopaths seem blessed with. The air conditioner was too heavy. The ashtray was vintage. I finally settled on a lamp, knowing it would be no match for his superhuman strength.

"Why?" Unlike most of my friends, Jo Ann took me seriously when I called to say for the fourteenth time that week that I had cancer. That's because she'd had it fourteen times that week too.

"I don't know. It's eerie, like nobody really lives here. There are sixty messages on his machine. Sixty. Exactly."

"Check 'em," she said firmly.

"I can't do that." I was still whispering. "What if he's in the bedroom right now getting messages from Plato and the Virgin Mary?"

"You'll just say you left his number with some people and you're checking to see if they called." Quick, decisive, a prizefighter of deception. I was usually not bad myself, but I was out of my element.

"I don't know."

"Do it," she ordered.

I crept with my phone cradled against me. My bedroom door, having read the script, squeaked ominously. I stopped, waiting for him to burst out of his room with a straight razor and a macabre laugh. Nothing. Nothing but that awful grove of silence.

"Where are you?" Jo Ann asked.

"Ssssshhhh . . ."

I walked in a peculiar, huddled fashion, which made me quieter and possibly invisible. When I got to the answering machine, I crouched and turned down the volume. At eye level were several doll-size gods made of coconut pieces painted primary colors. Their expressions were standard-issue gleeful/vengeful. God only knows what sacrifices they'd presided over.

I pressed rewind. The spinning cartridges whirred in my stomach. When the red numbers flicked down to twenty, I freaked, hit play, and caught the tail end of a Miss So-and-So from Citibank who could be reached at the following number until 5:00.

"Can you hear it?" I whispered.

"Yep," she said. She'd lit a cigarette. I could hear her smoking.

The next message was from his sister. John, please call, we're wondering how you are.

The next one was from Cablevision. They needed to talk to him about his bill.

Sis, again, this time a little more jollying, sort of come-out-come-out-wherever-you-are.

He needed to pay his phone bill or he'd only be able to receive calls.

Sister. Joking, but worried.

Then there was the electric bill.

Sister.

Citibank.

Sister.

A credit agency trying to fool him into phoning with a chummy little come-on. And that was the pattern. Sister, creditor, sister, creditor, sister, creditor. Dead silence from Jo Ann's end. Not even the sound of her smoking. I could see her cigarette, one long worm of ash, suspended in the air between her fingers. I could see her jaw on her clavicle. By the time we got up into the forties, each message was an ice-cold glass of cyanide-laced Kool-Aid cascading down my vertebrae. The sister tried, variously: cajoling, threats, entreaties, nonchalance, appeals to their shared past, bribery.

I told myself that I was a nervous Nellie who had often mistaken people for serial killers simply because they were inappropriately friendly or dressed in uninterpretable ways. Once, a man in a bar, who I'd known long enough to sip my beer, asked me to pretend that he was Axl Rose and I was Michael Jackson (I'm not black) and then we could go to his place and wrestle in a child's pool of baby oil, which apparently he kept at the ready in his living room. Then the winner would tie the loser up. Did I think I could beat him? I was almost sure about him; but generally I was content to be convinced by my friends that I was simply a borderline hysteric, that it wasn't mathematically possible that one out of four persons I met were psychopathic killers. Even a borderline hysteric could acknowledge those odds.

Expecting that same reassurance now, I said, admirably calm, "Maybe it isn't as bad as it sounds."

Have you ever heard hysterical laughter? Probably not. I'd

heard of hysterical laughter, but until you've been privy to the real thing, you will never know. It is high-pitched laughter to be sure, but indistinguishable from the sound a wildebeest makes on the Discovery Channel when it comes to the awful realization that that nice branch is actually a thirty-foot anaconda. That was the sound Jo Ann was making in my ear, hiccuping, "Oh, my God," when she could catch her breath. My heart NASCAR-Funny-Car-barrel-rolled in my chest.

The Twilight Zone of the messages finally ended. Jo Ann descended back from the helium of her laughter, and she did reassure me that he didn't sound like a serial killer. She was an avid fan of *COPS*, so I figured who would know better, right? But we both agreed that he was unstable, perhaps dangerously so. Not a tough call. Only another dangerously unstable person would think otherwise. I should move.

I should move; but I'd blown my wad on moving trucks and gay roommating services and trips back and forth to find a place to begin with and it seemed like every time I peeked through the curtains, another fifty dollars evaporated from my hand and all I had to show for it was a pack of cigarettes, a diet Coke, and some sparklers a guy in a knit cap was selling from a folding table on the street corner. I should move. But I'd only just gotten here yesterday. I'd quit my job and abandoned my boyfriend and moved out of our house after more talks than I could shake my broken heart at.

The last year was one long blur of me in bed watching the Home Shopping Network, at first conning myself that this was all sociological research for the masterpiece I was going to start writing as soon as I started writing again. There had been a time when I had written avidly, with the sort of idealism that didn't give two fucks about anything but itself. But a few bad breaks and a dash of bad luck, not helped by a lot of fair to poor writing, had cracked the spine of my will in several places, and at this point teams of specialists were working round the clock, wondering if I'd ever write again. That's really why I'd moved back, hoping that the invisible wires crisscrossing the city and coursing with energy would jumpstart my life again, most specifically, my writing life.

I couldn't go back to the Home Shopping Network, having given up the con that this was any sort of research. No, I'd actually started thinking, "Wow! That is a rock-bottom price for amethyst studs," and it was a short hop from there to calling friends and asking if I could use their credit cards to buy a four-hundred-dollar doll named Stevie, who was outfitted in genuine green velveteen britches! An Austrian lace collar and matching cuffs! He came with a certificate of authenticity! You could hear the exclamation points in Tina Berry's voice! My God! Why weren't the phone lines of the Home Shopping Network jammed? Except that they were, and I was trying to convince my friend Anne to help me jam them up further with all the other Home Shoppers out there, courtesy of Anne's MasterCard. She refused, she told me I needed help; and as I lay there, unshowered, the ashtrays surrounding me eensy burial mounds of crushed cigarettes, knowing that I'd empty those ashtrays and hop in the shower just minutes before Mark got home so he wouldn't know, I saw Stevie through her eyes (I'd told her to flip to it so she could see that I wasn't crazy) and I knew she was right. So I'd vaporized my life, and now I'd started another. Yes, I needed to move; but if it meant moving back to Richmond — and that's what it did mean — then whatever John was, he was stuck with me.

I guess it took me three weeks to find a catering job. In all that time I never saw John, or the alleged Alan, though I occasionally heard the sounds of humans moving furtively in the night. It was not reassuring, though Jo Ann did an admirable job of concocting perfectly ordinary explanations for why two people would all but abandon a two/three bedroom (Alan's quarters had been blocked out from part of the living room) apartment to me. In the afternoon, anything sounds plausible. The day is still filled with sunlight and possibility. Maybe they were just on vacation. But at 3:00 in the morning, when cabinets were clicking open and clicking shut in utter dark, every explanation ended in a homicide.

I'd worked in restaurants since I was fourteen, starting in the kitchen and finagling my way to the floor, where the real money was. I told my family, my friends from school, I told anyone who smiled down at me from the loft of their paid vacations and their health insurance that I did it so that I would have time to write, back when I did write. A half-truth, maybe more. Because being a waiter did force me to write — if I wasn't writing, then what the hell was I doing? I was waiting tables, that's what. I was waiting tables and I was out carousing with all the other misfits who found themselves in the restaurant business: the aspiring this-es, the given-up thats, the just-plain-couldn't-hack-its-in-the-real-world. But another part of the truth, which you could never admit to an outsider, was that I loved it when the vibe was good, when the owner wasn't a cokehead or martinet. I loved the speedy nights and the easy money and the strange hours. I loved the drunks and the crazies and the just-plain-couldn't-hack-its who staggered into the business; and they all eventually found their way to it, they all did. Prayer is not the last refuge of scoundrels; restaurants are.

And I'd gotten good. When I was twenty-seven, I'd lied my way into a French bistro, thinking I was ready to take the next step and go for the really big bucks. After one lunch, it became apparent to M. Alliman, the owner, that I didn't know how to serve bread from a basket with two soup-spoons — to cite one example — when a crusty French roll rocketed out of the rigor mortis of my grip and past the chignon of a woman who simply continued to sip her ver-mouth and converse in speed-of-light French with her equally unflappable companion, pausing only to brush the crumbs she knew must be there from the shoulder of her discreet silk blouse. She never even glanced at me. She didn't need to. M. Alliman could spot a salad fork one millimeter off its mark from ninety paces. I expected to be fired. I wasn't. It was one of those things that happens in restaurants sometimes. Some hard-ass decides you've got balls or promise or just wants to fuck you and suddenly you're in. M. Alliman did not want to fuck me. He already had a wife in a black leather miniskirt for that. But he was astonished that I would dare weasel my way into his restaurant — him, third-generation restaurateur — with the basest lies. It was beyond belief. Had I no idea who he was? Didn't I realize that this was a three-star restaurant?

Finally, once it was unequivocally established that he was French and I was the scum his chef skimmed from the fish stock, he allowed as how he sometimes admired a man who would dare such a thing. He ordered us lunch and two glasses of Alsatian wine and began to tell just such a tale about himself. Flourishes of the arms. Head thrown back in Gallic gales of laughter. So French I thought there'd be a Jerry Lewis film festival to follow. At the end of it all he clapped me on the back and said he was going to make me a "soljair in my army," that "here at La Gauloise, zee food is zee good news, and jou are zee apostle."

He spent the next year kicking my ass. I usually left my shift with shattered nerves, which I spit-pasted together with martinis until the next round; but by the time M. Alliman was done with me, I could have deboned Dover sole table side, served it to Charles Manson, and still gotten Charlie in a headlock if he got cute with me. Anyone who has ever worked in a restaurant has a story like that. It's called "How I Got My Chops."

All I'm really saying here is that I knew what I was doing. There was no reason why I couldn't waltz into Lutece or Chanterelle or Boulez, and then waltz out with Saturday nights in my back pocket. Actually, I knew better than that; and I was prepared to do my time in trenches of low-paying lunches and sanity-shredding brunches. If worse came to worse, I could get on with a caterer somewhere. Right? Wrong. To get on at a New York T.G.I. Friday's you had to have a doctorate in buffet tables, curly fries, and frozen-drink machines. I dutifully breaststroked my way through the swamps of August heat. I dutifully put together outfits that I hoped were two cups of professionalism and a soupçon of hip. I dutifully sat at the ends of bars filling out applications with my own pen, which I was always careful to bring. I went through the Yellow Pages calling caterers. When they didn't outright snort at me, they asked for a résumé, letters of recommendation, a passport, head shots, a Polaroid of me in my tuxedo, a DNA sample. The only one I'm kidding about is the DNA sample. Besides, even if I did have all that, they weren't hiring now anyway, though they might be in the fall, and what's more, no one ever left there, and even when they did, you had to call, like, that day, because when there was even a sniff of a job with them, the lines started forming in triplicate up and down Fifth Avenue, so I should really just keep calling back until something actually opened up, though they really didn't appreciate it when people bugged them like that, so I could call if I wanted to, but hey. Had I considered atom smashing or code breaking? They'd heard there was stuff open in that.

So I called everyone I knew and everyone they knew and I asked them if there wasn't someone I could bribe or blow into giving me a fucking waiting job. No, they didn't. They were sorry, but they hadn't done that sort of thing in years, having achieved their goal of being bloated with cash and self-satisfaction. A rich lady photographer I'd met at an artists' colony a few years back informed me that people were constantly calling her and asking her things like that, and she really resented it. In other words, though she refused to speak those exact words, she was tired of being hounded just because she was rich. Poor dear. I knew just how she felt. People were always hounding me too, and just because I was poor. Money, money, money was all those people ever thought about. They wanted it for food. They wanted it for lodging. They wanted the shirt off my back to pay for the shirt off my back. I didn't tell the rich lady photographer that she was the last person who I thought might know about a good catering gig, since her family name could be routinely found on endowed buildings scattered throughout the city, but that I had hoped she might bully one of the caterers she regularly employed into hiring me. But I'm always so stunned by the arrogance of the heedless rich toward the plight of the grasping poor — of which I was a card carrier — that I think I actually may have muttered that I was sorry. That's power.

Finally, some guy — God bless him — who was the fuck buddy of the cousin of a woman I met at the video store, something like that, thought he had, hold on, the card of a guy he used to cater for back when he was pathetic. Yeah, here it was. Dan. He lived in Brooklyn. After I called Dan two or three times a day for a week, he finally agreed to let me send him the usual portfolio. So I fabricated a résumé with tons of New York experience, forged letters of recommendation, borrowed more money from Jo Ann for the head shots, scrounged around for the passport, hair follicles for the DNA.

FedExed it. Sucker. He called the next morning wondering why I wasn't captain of the White House dining room. He had a job that very night. I was learning.

Dan turned out to be the kind of needlessly enthusiastic person who always seems on the verge of bursting into the school song. His lieutenants were only fractionally less ecstatic about pushing hors d'oeuvres. People designed to exhaust you. At least he didn't seem like a prick, though you never knew with these rah-rah types. Sometimes their pom-poms concealed switchblades. But despite the fact that he did things with his hands too much — clapping, rubbing them excitedly — he did have a big smile, and it was hard not to smile back. We scurried about, setting out dyed carnations, lighting candles under the steam trays, snapping open chairs. I went into my legendary impersonation of a person who liked nothing better than to make cloth napkins into interesting shapes, zipping around with the best of them, a smile chiseled over my lips. Not chiseled, exactly. I was, if not happy, then at least relieved to be making money; and that relief, after the last month, was a cozy sort of comfort.

They gave us half an hour to eat before the shift started: glops of pasta, drenched wads of salad, chicken that had been inadvertently baked into jerky, all of it slopped out by barely paid Hispanic cooks who spoke no English and actually seemed to know only three words in their native tongue — "hot," "whore," and "faggot." We devoured the food; it was free. One young woman fought her way back to the buffet pan to swipe up the last few smears of pasta sauce. She burned her finger, and even though she had to swish it in her glass of Sprite until the wedding guests began to trickle in, she seemed to think it was worth it.

It's hard when you're the new kid. Caterers, even nice caterers like Dan, expect you to whirl through the party, arms loaded with either bus pans or canapés at all times. They expect you to know where the paper doilies are stored and who Svetlana is. They expect you to know how to flambé when some wise guy yells, "Green card!" and the kitchen vamooses. They do not expect to have to tell you any of these things. They're too busy torpedoing past you braying orders and having nervous breakdowns because the bride wants to cut the cake and they can't find the sterling-silver cake knife — handed down through three generations of Weinbergs — that the mother of the bride entrusted them with a scant three hours ago, and have you seen it?

Oh, sure, before the lunatics are loosed on the asylum, they'll swing an arm around your shoulder and tell you that if you don't know where something is, just ask. If you don't know how it's done, no problem, it's your first night. Anything at all, don't hesitate. Filthy lies. Lie low, look busy, learn later: the beginner's motto. I knew that, but I also knew that I had been doing this, on and off, for the past twenty-two years. I could see that all the other waiters were about twelve, and I had listened to their eager-beaver talk over so-called dinner about auditions, about the studios they were sharing to make their art, about the classes with Merce, about how Grace Paley had said in their last workshop that they were a genius and how "Grae" was going to pass their collection, when it was done, on to her editor. I loved Grace Paley.

True, there was one poor dear who looked like she'd been summoned from the Cater Waiter's Crypt; and another fellow whose ruffles were stained, whose cheeks were neon from alcoholism, and whose mouth was set in a scowl lodged somewhere between rage and resignation. And, oh yes, one of the lieutenants was graying at the temples, but she smiled the secret smile of someone who'd never expected that much and had gotten it. I wasn't the only one, but I felt like the only one. At least the drunk seemed involved in the drama of destroying his life, and the Crypt keeper had a relationship with the Pall Mall Gold 100s she chain-huffed that looked stronger than most marriages. The lieutenant looked like she could have been a prison guard or the queen of Denmark and it wouldn't have mattered either way. I wanted to be her. If it didn't matter either way then I could have stayed in Richmond, working a couple nights a week in the restaurant, teaching the occasional class at the local university when the homophobes had run out of buddies to hire, not even trying to write anymore, just going shopping and eating toast until one day I died.

I was thirty-six. In less than four years I'd be forty. "Control Tower," a disco line dance, was playing over the loudspeakers. I was offering caviar on cream cheese in puff pastry from a silver doilied tray to babbling clots of strangers in clothes that cost more than I'd ever made my whole life. Dan was racing around on the diesel of an enthusiasm I didn't even have the fumes of, and quite suddenly, the guillotine of I-don't-think-I-can-bear-this-anymore chopped my head off.

Later, as we dragged ninety-pound marble cocktail tables up three flights of stairs, the twelve-year-olds leaping past me like fawns, I was almost certain I couldn't bear it anymore. And even later, as I leaned against a pillar in the subway station, the heat like glue, the noose of my loosened bow tie slung around my neck, as all the late-night hustlers and the other dubious characters eyed the damp cowl of my tuxedo, as the train thundered up and I swayed into it, I knew I couldn't take it anymore. I got back to the usual creepy quiet of John's and took the vodka bottle to bed. I sniffled to Jo Ann that I had to find another way to live. She must have said, "I know," about forty times. I said I was even willing to be the lady who handed out hot towels and spritzes of perfume in the bathroom at Macy's. Did she think they had that job anymore?

I finally drizzled off to sleep; but at some point I bolted awake into the cave of the middle of the night. Something calamitous was happening next door in John's room. He was coughing. But his coughing, compared to regular coughing, was the difference between a mosquito buzzing somewhere in the room to a 747 breaking the sound barrier right outside your window. It was epic coughing. It sounded like he was being clawed to death from the inside out. It did not sound survivable.

I sat up, my covers clutched in my hands, as if that could protect me. In the darkness, the shapes of my few things were beginning to assert themselves. Whatever drunk I'd tied on had completely unraveled. I was six-cups-of-coffee awake. My heart hummingbirded in my chest. It sounded like he was coughing up whole stretches of road and mountain ranges and dictatorships. Hot little tears began to bead in my eyes. It sounded like he was throwing up all the sorrows of the world. I rocked back and forth, hugging a pillow. My flimsy bookcases, my ancient computer on my desk, the tiny, tiny table piled high with stuff: in the dark it all looked like primitive groupings I'd pushed together that had failed to ward off evil. The end of the world was still at gale force next door. The paralysis bled from my brain. I had to help him. Of course. What the fuck was wrong with me? I got up, footed around for my underwear. Turning on the light seemed too gruesome. Whenever horrible things have happened near me, it's always the ordinariness going on and on and on around it that has killed me. Like my books just sitting there worthlessly on the shelf.

John had his own bathroom off his own bedroom, and he seemed to have made it there. His agony now had a tiled echo to it. I squeaked open my door, walked in that funny way that made me invisible, and stood outside his room, my hand poised and ready to knock. He seemed to be subsiding, little waves of whatever it was lapping through him. I decided to wait until he could hear me. It felt like one of the only times in my life when I was absolutely filled with what I was doing: waiting. My mind didn't wander. Nothing itched. I had achieved the kind of perfect attentiveness I'd heard my Buddhist friends go on about. As far as I was concerned, they could have it.

It seemed to be over, the Olympian event of his body. I tapped, lightly. I felt embarrassed to have overheard something so intimate and obscene. It seemed imperative, and also insane, to be polite. "John?" I tried.

Nothing except the trap of the apartment's silence, the grave of its dark. I tapped again, a little louder. "John?" A little more forcefully.

I waited again, but this time there was nothing perfect about it. My head was cyclonic with what I should do. Given my imagination, I was hurled from the cyclone to the conclusion that he was dead. It only took about three seconds, but in three seconds I had considered several thousand courses of action, including suicide, because the world was just too awful to live in. I officially knocked. "John." Urgent.

Again, nothing; and just as suddenly I was convinced that he was waiting too. I could feel it like a rope tied to both our waists, him there, exhausted in the dark, hugging the bowl, embarrassed too, maybe, not knowing me well enough to want to share whatever was happening to him, not knowing me at all, in fact, hoping, praying — I could almost hear the "Please, Gods" rowing around his head — that I would just go the fuck away so he could rest his cheek there against the cool porcelain, just that, that's all he wanted, if he could only have that then everything would be fine. I stood for one or two more eternal minutes, then drifted back to bed, too drained to even bother hunting down a Valium. An utterly dreamless sleep fell on me like a house.

I woke up at about 11:00 the next morning. TV burbled from the living room, the first normal sound I'd heard since I'd moved in. I pulled on a T-shirt and went to make coffee.

There sat John on one end of the couch, gaunt and white, with charcoal marks burned under his eyes. He looked like a gargoyle, posed with the remote in his hand, his long arms wrapped around his knees. A gargoyle in a Yankees baseball cap and a SYSCO T-shirt tented around him. On the other hand, he didn't look that different from most of the New Yorkers I knew. He turned, tilted his head, and high beamed a smile at me that was almost garishly big for how thin he was. That's when I knew he was sick, when his smile was too big for his face; and I assumed it was AIDS, even though he had offhandedly remarked during my interview that he was negative. Still, gay man, New York, early forties, looking not good. I knew the drill.

Really, I'd been remarkably lucky. I was negative. By some miracle, everyone I knew was negative. A barely functioning sex life, deformed or nonexistent social skills, simple timidity: something had saved us. By "lucky" I mean that I had only lost three close friends. By "lucky" I mean that I hadn't crossed out an entire address book. I knew people, and I'd heard of plenty more, who had.

"Hi," John said, too bright, more high beams.

"Hi," I said, a little more tentatively than I would have liked. "How are you?" From my tone, which I could not seem to get a grip on, I felt like I may as well have been asking if he was dying.

"Great." Chipper, somebody breezing by you at the office. "I love Bob Barker." He turned back to the hysteria of *The Price Is Right* and concentrated like it was the bar exam. The performance was over; it was all he could muster. I made coffee and padded back to my room. I've never been so studiously ignored. Five minutes later the no-longer-comforting sounds of the TV disappeared like they'd been karate chopped in the throat. John's door clicked open, clicked shut. Quiet reflooded the apartment.

That afternoon I found myself sitting in an office in Soho next to a woman named Tabitha who dressed like an ice-skater: metallic-looking leotard, dyed blond hair pulled back so tightly I thought her eyebrows would pop off, stage makeup. She was an aspiring actress, about twenty (though she was agelessly hard-bitten), and I had the feeling she'd be aspiring for some time to come.

There were other people sitting around waiting too, and there was a barbed-wire feeling of teeth-gritting determination in the air. We all felt that we had to have this job or die. Tabitha had said as much. Their outfits, mine included, looked mainly befuddled, like we'd all been dressed by children. It had been hard to guess what to wear. The ad had been one of those generalized ones that promised unheard-of wages for virtually no work. There had been talk of flexible hours, vague intimations of unspeakable glamour. It seemed to imply that the right person, a self-starter, a people person, could float to some unnameable top on mighty, mighty clouds of cash.

Anyone who knew me, starting with my mother, could have told you that I was not a self-starter or a people person. I usually couldn't find the ignition. Other people struck me as either terrifying or tragic. But since I couldn't program computers or design interiors or direct accounts, since I was not a laboratory histotechnologist, to name only one of the many things the *New York Times* Help Wanteds reminded me I was not, since I, more than anything, wanted out of the restaurant business, I was here. What I was was desperate and, in general, a good to excellent liar; but looking around me, I could tell that I had competition on both scores.

The office was militantly spare: plastic chairs for us to sit on, a girl at a desk paging through *Allure*. Everything was gray. The only signs of personality were the girl's Garfield coffee cup and the gigantic, luridly colored photograph thumbtacked to the wall, not of Garfield but of another kitty-cat in a ribbon with its head thrown back and a come-hither stare, a JonBenet of a kitty, kitty porn. It made me so nervous I could not look at it, even out of the corner of my eye. It seemed like more than a weird photograph. It seemed like the end of civilization. I talked nonstop to Tabitha so I wouldn't think about it. She confided to me that people had told her she looked like Princess Di. Then she made me run lines with her for an audition she had right after this. I played a psychiatrist. She played a woman who was going to a psychiatrist. I developed an accent and my own motivation for the scene. Tabitha, who wasn't easily impressed, was, and suggested that I take classes with her at HB Studios. In the middle of my acceptance speech for Best Supporting Actor, which seemed realistic given that I was probably more of a character actor, a man erupted from the door behind the desk. He was good-looking, with brambly, black hair, and his confidence whacked you from thirty paces. He scanned the dozen or so applications on the desk, frisbeeing most of them to the floor. Then he barked out four names: mine, Tabitha's, two other gaping people.

We stood up and walked, hypnotized, toward the open door, behind which Barry — that turned out to be his name — had already disappeared. The other contestants were gathering up their backpacks and grumbling. The girl behind the desk continued to gaze vacantly at models whose lips looked fatter than their thighs. In a way, they reminded me of John.

We, the elect, sat down in four more plastic chairs. Barry's office was as barren as the rest of the place, except for one extravaganza of a mahogany desk importantly messy with papers. He leaned back in his chair, his fingers templed under his nose, studying us like bugs that had inconveniently smacked against his windshield, a movie pose, really, a pose Dale Carnegie's evil twin would have taught to up-and-coming corporate raiders. I relaxed. Even if he was serious, he had to be kidding.

Barry suddenly pushed back his wheeled throne and jumped onto the desk. The importantly messy papers scattered like storks sensing an alligator on the Discovery Channel. He made jazz hands and said, "Are you prepared to do this? If this is what it takes?"

Well, it was startling. The other two were saucer-eyed. I could feel that my own eyebrows had met with my forehead.

Only Tabitha was unimpressed. She sat there, leg crossed over metal-looking leg, like pylons. Defiant chin in bored palm. "Yeah," she said. "What for?"

He lowered himself into a sitting position on the edge of the desk, jeaned ankles crossed and swinging, your basic kid on bridge with fishing pole. "Aaaahhh, but that wouldn't be any fun if I told you, would it?"

"Whatever," Tabitha said.

"This is the kind of job where you've got to be prepared to do anything to get, and to keep, people's interest."

"I'm an actress," Tabitha said flatly.

"It's not glamorous. But it is an opportunity. A potential fucking gold mine. And you guys would be getting in on the ground floor."

Beside me, I thought I could feel Tabitha rolling her eyes, but she said, "Sounds interesting," and it sounded like she meant it. She was either a lot more gullible than I'd given her credit for, or a lot more talented.

"What about you two?" he commanded, pointing with his whole arm at them. They clutched the sides of their plastic chairs and nodded sures, yeahs, uh-huhs, and one absolutely.

"And you?" He cocked a finger at me.

"Sure. Why not?" I'd calmed back down. Unless the moon was dyed the red of blood and the sun now set in the east, there was no way that my nervous system would allow me to even consider a job like this, whatever it was. I was not the type to jump on desks. I was more the type to hide under them.

26

"You don't sound very sure there, uh, what's your name again?"

"Wesley."

"Right. Gibson. You don't sound so sure there to me, Gibson."

Oh, so he was one of those drill sergeants who called you by your surname. Got it. "Look," I said, rotten with confidence now that I knew this job and I were star-crossed. "I had to hold the attention of a bunch of bored twenty-year-olds when I taught college. I guess I can do this."

"You taught college, huh?" he said, pouting out his lower lip and nodding his head like, hey, pretty impressive.

I was suddenly embarrassed. "It wasn't . . . all that," I said, wondering when I'd started talking like a Ricki Lake audience.

"OK," he said, giving us a final once-over, "you guys seem OK to me, even you, Professor."

Professor. What a fraud. I'd taught adjunct creative writing in a third-rate English department. I winced and turned it into a tight, little smile. "So," I had to know, particularly since I'd never be back, "what are we being hired to do again?"

"Two words. Comedy clubs. And that's all I'm going to tell you. Everybody be back here at eight-thirty sharp. If you're one second late, don't bother."

He hopped off the edge of the desk and up-upped with his hands. Now we slung on our own backpacks, not really looking at one another as we did, like we'd all been a part of something shameful, a circle jerk, an Avon party. Once again I was projecting, at least as far as Tabitha was concerned. She stuck out her hand and he shook it. "I like you," she said.

I continued to struggle with my backpack, which had turned into a cat's cradle. The other two slinked out. Tabitha strode. "Hey, Professor," Barry said, putting his cute hand on my unemployed shoulder, then latching on to me with his even cuter brown eyes. Serious gaze à la camp counselor in a Lifetime Original Movie. "What are you doing here, man?"

"I need a job."

"This is not for you."

"I need a job." All my bravado about not being able to jump on desks steamed away. Even if I couldn't do a job in which I had to possibly make jazz hands, it suddenly seemed vital that he at least think I could. If I could trick him into seeing me as a people person, a person with spunk and initiative, real drive, then maybe I could fool others too. If not, if I couldn't pull off this one minor deception, then I was headed down the chute that led to the bottle-strewn gutter. So I stared back, equally serious, the kid at the camp who had heard him, man, and was now showing his cards too, all of them, faceup, no more bullshit. "I want this job."

Another shoulder pat. Tentative smile. "OK, man," he said. "OK. I'm going to give you a shot."

"You won't regret it," I bald-faced lied, breaking into a Super Bowl of a smile.

"Get out of here," he said, giving me an affectionate shove toward the door.

Yes, it was true, we'd bonded as superior beings, me with all my book learning, him with his street smarts. What a team we'd make, me his second-in-command, as we moved the offices into increasingly impressive digs and I convinced him to get rid of that kitty photograph. Eventually, of course, he'd realize that he loved me, and he'd understand when, increasingly, I'd have to spend time at our place upstate on the Hudson to pursue my artistic passions, until one day he died. Sure, I'd go on, I might even be seen out in the company of desirable young men, but I'd never really love again.

I never got that job. I overslept. For two very bad reasons. The first is that I have, as relates solely to myself, telekinetic powers on a par with Carrie's. If I'm afraid that I won't sleep and the alarm won't go off and even if it does then there won't be any hot water to shower with, then it happens. My fear wills it to happen. Some university should do a study on me.

The second, far worse reason was that when I finally did jitter asleep, John woke me up again. The astonishment of his coughing. The bears of his retching. I could hear him pushing his face into his pillow so I wouldn't hear. It didn't work. What was happening was too terrible, too discordant, the body in the full throttle of its own unmaking. I sat up again. I hugged my own pillow and rocked again. I watched my things there in the dark gather shape and volume and take on the strange weight of actually being my things as whatever was wrong with John marauded through him. It must have gone on for forty-five minutes, an hour, as little by little I made my way toward his room, pausing when he paused, pushed forward when he was ambushed again, eventually standing there in front of his door — it was like standing on a disappearing island — finally knocking once and saying his name, loud enough so that I was sure he could hear me. Nothing. When the next cataclysmic bathroom echo sounded, I could tell that he had buried his face in his arm to mute it. It was like holding up a twig to fight off the storm. Clearly he wanted me not to be there. Maybe he wanted to believe that nothing was really wrong with him — I could understand that — and I could also understand how my concern was probably making that hard for him. But I couldn't just go about my business, I couldn't. I also suspected that a sensible person, a finer person, would have already broken down the door and dragged him to a hospital. But I wasn't even sure about that. So all I did was stand there, listening with all my might for any sign that maybe it was time for the rescue operation, and it didn't help either of us.

The next day, I woke up at 11:00. TV sounds again; and sure enough, there was John at his self-appointed place: same Bat time, same Bat channel. He slugged me with that smile. It was beyond odd. I'd never seen someone smile who so didn't mean it. It was like the smile of an inanimate object. "This woman," he said, "you wouldn't have believed it. She kept crying and crying. She won these CD box sets, and then she won a car, and she kept crying and crying. It was so cute. She lost on the Big Wheel, though." He turned back to the squealing and the dinging.

I didn't know what to say so I said, "Wow." Then I stood there idiotically. John rubbed his thumb across the bottom of the remote. He was wearing a crystal around his neck. He yawned. I'd been disappeared again.

"Do you have a cold or something?"

"No." He didn't like that one bit. I could feel him refusing to look at me.

"Oh." I scratched my right foot with my left big toenail. "It's just you sound stuffed up or something." Maybe that was what he'd tell himself later, that he'd caught some summer bug. Maybe that's what he was already telling himself.

Nothing.

I made coffee in the machine I'd dragged down from Richmond. The brightly colored bedlam of *The Price Is Right* was interrupted by a commercial for *Cats,* now and forever, which sounded like a threat to me, and by one for insurance that covered your "final expenses" so you wouldn't be "a burden to your loved ones." The machine peed out my coffee. I dragged my hand through my hair and decided I needed to cut my toenails, which were good for scratching, but basically a menace. The smell of the coffee was almost soothing, but not quite, not with John sitting behind the wall rigidly pretending that nothing was wrong, and me wondering if I should tell him there was. If he just could have committed to a cold, then maybe I could have too. I was perfectly willing to deceive myself for his benefit, but he was going to have to give me a little something to go on.

But he didn't. I leaned against the kitchen doorway, sipping my coffee. I offered a guess as to the price of a sailboat. He was granite. After several minutes oozed by like old honey, I gave up and returned to my room, shutting the door on Bob and John. The TV died immediately. After what seemed like too long, he made it back to his room. These little performances must have been life draining, and as I considered that, the world seemed like a horrible, boulder-strewn place.

And that's how it went for the next few days. Nights of the living dead; midmornings of them too, in which I got to see the cast out of makeup, just a regular guy in a baseball cap who watched game shows. Some tidbit from John about the high jinks blasting from the tube. Me standing around alternatively suggesting that some pretty terrible flus were going around out there, or taking a crack at how much an iced-tea maker might go for. John's silence.

Fortunately, Jo Ann was on her way. She'd know what to do.

I don't remember anymore how long it had been since Jo Ann had been to New York, but it seems like it had been a long time because I had to meet her at the bus station, something I would have done only for my family, who thought New York was nothing but a concrete island of murderers and the people who loved them.

Naturally, I'd gotten fucked up about where we were supposed to meet. *Post* headlines about her disappearance scrolled through my head. I saw the grainy blowup of a photograph they'd scanned from her high school yearbook. But then, strolling through the zigzag of people preoccupied with where they needed to be, yesterday, I saw her — big, black bag hoisted over her shoulder, big, genuine smile on her face. How happy was I to see her? As happy as that guy with the broken leg on the edge of the cliff when Lassie finally shows up with the park ranger.

We hugged, hard, and I asked her how the Greyhound trip was. "The usual serial-killer convention," she said. It was almost frightening how similarly our minds worked.

I don't remember how we got home. For some reason it feels like it was the subway because I have a distinct memory of wrists with gold bracelets, and the stubble above the suit of some guy who was past tired, and a crumpled coffee cup with QUARTERS drilled into it with a Bic pen. The usual body-part sightings of any subway ride. Whatever we took, it was not life affirming. By the time we staggered past the doorman and rode up the elevator with an Asian family who looked like they'd just flown in from a Gap ad, by the time we got back to the clobbering silence of John's, our spirits had been crushed, along with our wills.

Jo Ann flopped backfirst on the bed and lit a cigarette. Then she propped her head on the triangle of her arm and had a real look around. "This is nice," she said, with complete conviction. I looked around too: the stark, curtainless windows; the walls that had aged from their original white to some unnameable pastel; IKEA-esque — and wasn't that esque sad — bookcases; an unpainted bed with drawers underneath that I'd bought from Gotham Cabinetmakers; art by my friends, none of whom were Willem de Kooning. Jo Ann was quite a little actress. She left Tabitha in the dust.

"No, it's not," I said.

"Some curtains," she conceded. "A little table right here." She gestured beside the bed. "The desk is great."

The desk *was* great: blond wood, black iron boomerang legs, a gold-flecked Formica top.

"Let's go shopping," she said.

"Uh, I don't really have any money."

"Housewarming present."

"I've already borrowed too much from you."

"You need curtains."

I needed my pride, but looking at the blank faces of the windows, I decided I needed curtains more.

There's a saying in New York that if you're one in a million there are still ten more just like you. And that's exactly right. It isn't so much that there's too much of everything, though there's certainly that, it's that there's not one of anything. That may seem like a hairsplitting distinction, but it's not. One of something is an oasis for the senses, even though everything else may be kaleidoscoping around it. One of something is a rest stop for the mind, however fleeting. When there's never one of anything, then there really is too much of everything. It's a twenty-four/seven shift with no coffee break, no lunch, no refreshing trips to the watercooler. Even Central Park is too much. Most parks are like movie librarians before they let their hair down: discreet, unassuming, whisperingly helpful. Not Central Park. Central Park is Martha, as in George and Martha, braying at you, "I do not bray." It's too much of muchness.

Eventually, you adapt. One evening you're hanging on to a subway ring during rush hour. You're reading a magazine with the other hand. You scratch your nose with the magazine, look into someone's armpit stain, and you think, hmmm, this isn't so bad. I'm not saying that's a good thing. In fact, I'm almost sure that it's not. But it's a necessary mutation for survival. On this day I'm talking about, though, I was still a relatively normal person with the usual sensitivity to people yelling and thinking it was talking, to odd pockets of rotting smells for no apparent reason, to bizarre little coincidences like six nail salons in the same block. Jo Ann had just come from an apartment with a huge porch that overlooked a lake, so I could just imagine.

We'd only been about three blocks when I said, "What's your level?"

"Six." She paused. "Six and a half," she said, upgrading.

"Me too," I said.

We were talking about our anxiety. Six, six and a half wasn't bad. But seven was, so we were close. Eight was definite trouble. Nine was still pretty much theoretical. Ten was the last moments before your plane smacked into the water. Three to five was just life.

I should add that it was bright white out, hot like that.

"Why don't we stop in here?" she said about a store with decent-looking furniture in its massive windows. I couldn't tell if it was to level off or because she'd seen something worth inspecting.

The store was cool, shadowed; and the furniture, though

of course there was too much of it, didn't look bad, sort of sleek and modern and black with rounded edges. A person with some money and some taste could have fixed up his joint real snazzy. I wasn't that person, but it couldn't hurt to browse.

We looked at curvy CD holders, and blond-wood tables that stacked neatly on top of one another. Cute retro footstools in hunting-lodge burgundies. In Richmond, there wouldn't have been enough of a market for these guys to have rented a storefront; but here, there were enough people who might buy a dresser with brushed aluminum handles in the shape of quotation marks or sperm that this place was as big as a supermarket. Testing out chairs that looked like they couldn't possibly be comfortable — then turned out to fit you like a glove — I thought this truly seemed like a city where you might meet John Kennedy Jr., then marry him.

"You really need this," Jo Ann said, picking up a black rubber trash can that came up to my knee. It looked like it should have been in MoMA.

"Nah."

"It's only five dollars," she said, handing it to me. "You know, that little table over there would be nice too. With this on top." She picked up a place mat, also made of rubber, but multicolored. It looked like smashed crayons, in a good way. "We can cut it to fit."

"I don't know, Jo Ann. I don't really feel —"

"You need this stuff," she said, picking it up. "It's only fifteen dollars."

"But it's your fifteen dollars."

"I'll put it on my credit card. That's not real money. It's magic."

Also magical was that when we left, we seemed to have leveled off at about two. One, like nine, was still pure theory, possible only for people who were childlike as a result of catastrophic brain trauma.

That night we lay on my bed, smoking contentedly and watching *The Stepford Wives*, which we'd rented, lazily forking in delivered Thai food and comparing stomachs to see who was the fattest. There was no clear winner, as we'd both made excellent cases. We may have laughed a lot or we may not have. It all depended. At about midnight I offered to make up the couch in the living room for her. She said she'd rather sleep on a sewage grate than be defenseless and asleep out there in the wilds and weirdnesses of John's apartment. It was the first time either of us had seriously mentioned IT. I think we both knew there'd be plenty of time for that. Later.

Which there was. If John's illness didn't punch a clock, it did lurch into the apartment at about the same time every night. The red numbers of my alarm clock glowed 3:12 from my new Jo-Ann-bought table. I didn't sit up, the way I usually did, and Jo Ann didn't either. We both just lay there, unmoving, listening to the assault. It was even darker with my new curtains, though an aluminum take-out container began to vibrate faintly with light from my desk. Almost to twinkle. The room was fat and humid and oppressive with our lying there and not saying a word. The armed and dangerous troops of whatever it was pushed their relentless way through John, sending him on his nightly — and it sounded like, stumbling — trip to the bathroom. That awful echo. I could hear Jo Ann breathing. I could feel her lying there not moving. When there was finally a lull in the hideous festivities, I whispered, "What do you think?" still hoping, I guess, for some story about one of her cousins who'd coughed like that and how it had turned out to be nothing but a hair ball.

"You've got to do something," she whispered back. It was a plea, not a direct order.

So. It was as bad as I had thought. When was I going to get to the part where it wasn't as bad as I thought? You heard stories about that all the time. "Now?" I whispered.

"Nooo . . ." she said, drawing the word out uncertainly. "Not now. It's too late, he's too sick. But the next time you see him during the day, you really need to. He's dying."

I knew she was right, but I couldn't help but feel like all the presents she'd bought me were nothing but the ice-cream sundae before they tell you the dog died. I'd wanted a witness, to make sure this wasn't simply more of my making cancer cells out of the molehills on my arms, that it wasn't more of my revising the shadows on the walls into vampire bats. And now I had it. That was a definite relief. Anything was better than the waiting and the listening and the unanswered knocks. Anything was better than more *Price Is Right*.

But how did you do that? How did you go up to a stranger, not a perfect stranger, but an imperfect one, one made imperfect by proximity? How did you approach that imperfect stranger with such unglad tidings? Hi, uh, I know we don't really know each other all that well, but I, uh, I think you're dying. Particularly when you knew that person probably would rather die than face it. Where was that in all your books on gracious living, Martha fucking Stewart?

"I need my asthma inhaler," Jo Ann said. "No, don't turn on the light. I can find it in the dark."

Fortunately Jo Ann also agreed that while she was there was not the right time. A governor's stay. Our own books of ungracious living told us that if he didn't want one stranger knowing, he sure as hell didn't want two. So we rehung my art according to Jo Ann's taste, which made it look like the real art it was and not just stuff your artist pals had slipped you. We rented more movies and smoked quantities of cigarettes and ordered more delivered oriental food, of which there was an astonishing variety, and which made the upheaval of my move seem almost worth it. We did not go to the Met or to smoky jazz temples where it sounded like they were playing geometry equations. We did not find ourselves, after-hours, at smart little boîtes with booths of hangers-on draped over our shoulders. We battened down the hatches. We basically stayed put. Our anxiety levels stayed in the two to fives. Except at around 3:00 in the morning when we were hurled awake by John's billboard-size memo that life was a nasty business, brimming with death, even here in the city where people paid to hear geometry played. Except that his fits and seizures weren't confining themselves to the hollows of the night anymore. They were clawing their way into the thickly textured comfort of the daylight, where the men with briefcases and the languid women with cell phones six floors below on the sidewalk could almost convince you that death was nothing but a bogeyman, something in a book some bad man had drawn to scare the children.

Jo Ann saw him maybe twice. The first encounter was one magpie of a performance in which he offered to show us how the couch unfolded, did we have extra sheets, was she having a good time, could she believe the price of the exercise bike he was watching on TV, oh him, never mind, he just wanted to hear all about her. I wished I'd had an Academy Award in my back pocket. It was one for the ages. The second was a phone-in. John. TV. Comment about TV.

When Jo Ann left, she said, "You've got to do this."

I knew. I was ready. The next morning, I promised. I'd call and tell her what happened. When this was all over, could she — and at this point I'd accepted that this could only end badly — a) lend me five thousand so I could start all over again, b) let me come and live in her apartment overlooking the lake where I'd sit in a rocker on the porch with a comforter folded over my lap in deference to my slight chill, or c) put a violent end to my misery with something from the arsenal the NRA had made so readily available to ordinary citizens like ourselves. She chose d) all of the above, though she was unnervingly enthusiastic about c), saying that *They Shoot Horses, Don't They?* was one of her favorite movies.

The next day, J-Day, I woke up to the sounds of bustling. I rubbed the Jell-O from my eyes and leaned over to see that it was 8:30. I was not ready. I'd had the usual John-induced sleep, three hours pre–cough-echo-vomit, three post. It was not refreshing. But maybe it was Alan, dear, sweet, alleged Alan, and maybe he could shed some light on all this. Maybe he'd be willing to have that death chat with John himself. Alan had, according to John, lived here for going on two years. I fumbled into some clothes and pressed my hair down so I wouldn't look like a complete maniac as I tried to explain that we needed to intervene. It wasn't just me. Jo Ann had been here. She thought so too.

But it wasn't Alan. It was John, in sparkling white Nikes; pressed, stonewashed jeans; a polo shirt; and that Yankees baseball cap. Dressed, scurrying down the hall with a brown bottle of vitamin C in his hand, he looked like your average Joe, or John, off to a happy hour where they had steam trays of buffalo wings and women who teased their bangs. He didn't seem sick at all. He seemed energetic and purposeful, not like the 911 call waiting to happen that he'd been three hours ago. He snuggled the vitamin C jar into a floral-printed suitcase that sat openmouthed on the couch where he was usually curled up, close-lipped. He slapped it shut, zipped it with one quick, efficient sweep of the arm, then barreled down on me with that smile of his. Except this time he didn't seem to be faking it. He looked like a real, thin, happy, pale person, not the fakes of that person he'd been palming off on me for the last week, or was it two?

"Uh, where are you going?" I asked.

"To the hospital," he said, still smiling.

A river of relief, with gentle eddying currents, poured through me. "Oh, John, I'm so glad to hear that, man, I mean, I gotta say, you know, I was gonna talk to you this morning, cause, you know, it sounded kind of bad there for a while."

He smiled at me for a few more of those seconds that I'd become best buds with here lately — taffy, stretching seconds from another dimension where they were still working out time's kinks. Then he grimaced, seemingly at himself. "I know. The coughing, the gagging but inability to vomit, the black, tarry stool. According to my medical books, I probably have bleeding ulcers."

"Your medical books?" I probably should have expressed some concern over his condition, but John was always tackling the appropriate response from me with some unexpected development.

"Yes," he said crisply. "I'm a nurse."

"Nurse," I repeated like a child who would then say all the other new words he'd learned: doggie, mommy, boo-boo.

"I called one of the doctors I worked, work, with, and he's got me checked into Cabrini. He said I'll probably only be there for a few days so they can run some tests." He picked up the suitcase.

"Do you want me to, um, I don't know, do something?"

"Can't think of anything."

"I'll stop by and see you."

"Not necessary. It's just a checkup. I don't really like visitors at the hospital anyway. It's distracting."

I'd thought that was the point, but in another way, I knew what he meant. When I'd been in the hospital for an appendectomy, all I'd wanted was my TV and the drugs that made all shows, from the WWF to NOVA, deeply absorbing in a personal way not easily shared with others.

"OK, then."

"I'm off." And he was, making tracks like a snake-oil salesman with the town fathers on his tail. The front door whooshed open, slammed shut. The various dead bolts clicked back to locked with tiny sounds like a mouse chewing.

Well. There. See. Let that be a lesson to me. AIDS. It was nothing but little bleeding ulcers. And him a nurse. I guess he'd know when it was and when it was not time to get to the hospital. It was the same old, same old, the pentimento of my fear layering and layering itself over the tranquil seascape until I had a full-blown, storm-tossed Turner. Well. All I could say was that I hoped I'd learned a little something about the value of not being so spooked by what was just the regular stuff of life, and also taking bulls by horns, and maybe something about a couple of other things too while I was at it. Yeesh. It was about time I shaped up.

When I called to tell Jo Ann, she said, "Hmmmm . . . maybe," like someone who was willing to consider UFOs for the sake of humoring you. But not really.

John's several days turned into a week, and it was the best week I'd had since I'd moved there, a little over a month ago. It was like I was the one, not John, who was recovering from an illness, and I had all of the recoveree's heightened senses and exalted oaths to stop being dead to this carnival called life. It was time to hang from the horses of the carousel by one arm. It was time to go for that giant stuffed teddy bear. I called friends I'd been neglecting. I went to a reading of three very famous essayists at KGB, something I could never have done in Richmond; and it really and truly didn't matter when two of them were so in love with the sound of their own voices that they read for more than an hour apiece. What — under ordinary circumstances — would have been a pummeling reminder of writers and the freak-show gigantism of their egos was still a lovely evening of Russian vodka and warm companionship. It seemed touching that two people who made a living off their penetrating insight had so little when it came to themselves. I could afford to be generous.

I went to the park. It was September, still warm. Lovers gamboled. Heart stoppingly beautiful young men tossed different shapes of balls at one another with their shirts off. Babies, dappled in light sprinkling through leaf-fattened trees, stared wonderingly from their strollers at the birds and the bees, at their own slobbery little fists. A person could learn a lot from them about innocence and experience, about how it was possible to be both fat and still cute as a button. I lay there, splendid in the grass, little molecules of melanoma not forming on my pale skin. I read, not Pauline Kael's *5001 Nights at the Movies* for about the five-thousand-and-first time, but books I should have read by now and had intended to before the Home Shopping Network had destroyed my mind: Gaston Bachelard's *Poetics of Space,* a selected poetry and prose of Alexander Pope, another go at Sartre's *Saint*

Genet. This was who I had intended to be all along, before I'd been sidetracked by . . . what? Good question. Problem was, I didn't know the answer. Congenital despair? Crippling lethargy? Simple sloth? Maybe I'd never know. The point was that I was here, finally becoming the person I'd set out to be. I held my Bachelard in the air in hopes that one of the shirtless young men was sexually ambivalent and intellectually pretentious. One in a million? That still meant there were ten of him.

I even started to write. Well, my version, anyway. I turned on my computer. I wiped the dust from its screen with a sock lying conveniently nearby on the floor near the wheels of my chair. That led me to believe that the little ledge of shelf peeping out from under my books in the bookcases needed attention too. I didn't remove all the books and then swab down the entire shelf. That was the kind of crazy procrastination I refused to indulge in. But I did realize afterward that I needed a cup of tea, and that led me to the open living-room window, where I listened to the soothing thrum of the traffic. I tried to see if the couple across the way was fucking, something they did from time to time with the blinds thrown open in the overlit movie set of their bedroom. I figured they wanted an audience, and I was usually more than happy to oblige them. It passed the time. But when the good-for-nothings proved to be a no-show, again, I was finally forced to wander back to my desk, but not before I examined my gums in the bathroom mirror. I thought I'd tasted blood and wondered if I had pyorrhea. I couldn't decide about the pyorrhea, so I finally opened one of the many files containing the endless versions of my so-called novel, and it turned out that there were some commas that needed changing and even a couple of words, and then I got this nifty idea for how to save the whole shebang, which had something to do with a sort of magic realist thing, comic, but also deeply fraught with significance, which later turned out to be the worst idea I'd ever had. Still, it was something.

And I found a job, and not in a restaurant.

Telemarketing. It has that ring to it, that ring at dinner, that ring in your ear of someone's voice when they're finished shouting, that ring of the receiver being slammed back into the cradle. I never did that. I was unfailingly polite when MCI called for the sixth time that day, like a boyfriend gone stalker, to wonder why, oh, why had I decided to go back with Sprint? How could I do that to them? Didn't I know what I'd meant to them? I was polite because I knew that on the other side of the vast distance separating his cubicle from my living room was a poor sap trying to scrape by. That sap had been me and my friends. I remember Anne weeping into her bourbon after a night of asking people a complicated series of questions designed to discover why they used a certain deodorant, a brand of canned ravioli, different pens. It wasn't the questionnaire she minded; it was the rejections. She took them personally.

Anne, though she seems perfectly normal to me, is a large and eccentric woman who had escaped from her small town to become a lesbian and an English major. Two stories here. One, she was beaten up weekly at her Brownie meetings by an eleven-year-old who roared up on the back of her boyfriend's Harley wearing a black leather miniskirt. You'll say she's kidding, but I've been to that town. She's not kidding. Two, she once told a customer at the Dairy Freeze, when he asked to speak to the manager, that he couldn't because they were a socialist collective. While he was hunting around the back of his truck for his deer rifle, she hotfooted it out the back way. She was fourteen. Where Anne was from, you didn't kid about commies. Every night she spent at Marketing Associates was a concentrated tablet of the past. She hadn't liked those people from her town; but they hadn't liked her either, and there'd been more of them than there had been of her. The gals and guys bellowing no in her ear every night were some smudged mimeograph of the hecklers who'd done the same thing back in mythical high school. So she cried, she had a couple of drinks, and the next night she went back and did it all over again.

My own telemarketing job had been even worse. I'd been in college, and I think I found the job in this loose-leaf binder at the student center. I'm sure that the job description was like the jazz-hands gig — big bucks, "ideal for student." I showed up at around 6:00 in the evening. A bland brick building, the kind of place that had driven Willie Loman to commit suicide. A flight of steps covered in the kind of grimy rubber I associated with car mats. At least it was air-conditioned. Outside, the sweating fist of a Richmond summer was trying to choke the life out of you. There was no interview. I signed something that looked more like a disclaimer than an application. Some guy with algebra-teacher glasses and a clip-on shoved me into a cubicle, saying, "Those are the numbers and that's the script." He meant the two sheets of paper on either side of the phone.

"Script?"

"Yeah, script. You call the numbers and you read the script. A moe-ron could do it."

Yes, but what about a person with stage fright? What about a guy who'd forgotten all his lines as Benvolio, ruining the school play? What about a guy whose legs Charlestoned when he had to recite up in front of French class? Hey, mister . . . But Mister had stomped off, leaving behind him a rank smell of Right Guard and commerce.

I picked up the script. Who knew? Maybe without an audience I was a regular Robert De Niro.

Good evening, Mr./Mrs./Miss , this is , calling for Childcare (or whatever it was), and I was wondering if you'd like to sponsor a group of mentally and physically disabled children to go to the circus. For as little as one hundred dollars you could send up to twenty-five children with disabilities to the Wild Bill Family Circus. That's right, up to twenty-five children . . .

Etc.

My cubicle would have made a prison cell look overdecorated. All around me students were murmuring, except for one guy who was projecting to the third balcony. "MRS. PERKINS. BILL HERE, FROM CHILDCARE. ISN'T IT A SHAME ABOUT DISABLED CHILDREN? WOULDN'T IT

BE NICE IF WE . . ." A real actor, the kind of guy who was going to end up in an amusement park *biergarten* wearing lederhosen and singing "Edelweiss." I refused to think about my own prospects.

I hung up on my first three calls, waiting the third time until a woman was finally saying, "Chuck, is that you? I know it's you, Chuck. I've told you, this is over. Do —" I crossed my arms over my desk and laid down my head. It was dark there. I wondered if there was a Coke machine somewhere in this science project, like that pellet rats get for being Pavlovian. Tap on my shoulder. Couldn't be good. I turned around, trying to look like a person too valuable to fire, then remembered what I did look like: shoulder-length hair, earring, canary-yellow overalls. In Richmond, in 1978, a mood ring was considered daring.

"Hey, this isn't getting the job done." Clip-on again. Did I mention he had sideburns the size of Florida, polka-dotted with acne?

"I was, uh, resting. I already called, like, six people."

"Any sales?"

"One lady said to check back."

"You get a break at eight."

"Is there a Coke machine around here?"

"Down the street at the Hess station."

"Welp. Back to work." I swiveled around and moved my finger six places down my list. I shook out my script and cleared my throat impressively. Dialed. Listened to Sideburn's loafers thump down the slender corridor.

OK. I had to do this if I wanted to stand around the Dial Tone, the local gay bar, also known — and not for nothing — as the Busy Signal, drinking beers, playing pinball, and opening the door to my mystery dates. That cost money. So did cigarettes. So did the ingredients for a week's worth of chili and the occasional impulse buy. My needs were simple, but they weren't scot-free.

"Uh, hi, Mrs. Dandridge. Is that how you say it?"

Five-minute dissertation on the origins of her name in a vibratoed, ancient voice. She was southern, so I had to hear about all her great-great-cousins on her mother's sister's side who'd fought in the Battle of Bull Run during the "wo-wah." All these dragons called it the "wo-wah," and you knew exactly which wo-wah they meant. Me, checking my nails for dirt, then biting them off in delicate slivers. Neat pile of off-white crescents by the place where I tapped my pen.

"Yeah, wow, that's great. Hey, listen, how would you like to send some, like, retarded kids and stuff to the circus?" I'm sorry, I just couldn't stick to the script. I was more of a method telemarketer. "You would? Great. What should I put you down for? Well, let's see. There's a hundred-dollar level, a two-fifty, the golden circle but that's like a thousand. I guess you couldn't really be a corporate sponsor. Hundred dollars, huh? Great. Let me make sure I've got all your stats right here."

Hey, this was easy. It was too easy. Except for one woman whose husband had got his hand caught in the thresher and couldn't send her own "goddamned kids to the circus," they were all nice and accommodating. And old. I talked to more hearing-wrecked ladies than you could shake a social security check at about their cats and their Civil War dead. And they coughed it up too. All you had to say was "retarded," "kid," "circus," and the next thing you knew they'd walkered over, broken out the magnifying glass, and read me the numbers off their dead husbands' MasterCards. I didn't know about target marketing, but even a moe-ron could see that this was no random list.

Clip-on sneaked up and leaned over my shoulder to check my progress, his sideburn uncomfortably close to my temple. Something about him felt contagious. I tried to lean away, but that only sent me into the crook of his bare arm. "Good work," he said, grabbing my shoulder and giving it a meaty shake. His breath smelled like chewing gum and eighteen-hour days.

"Uh, what kind of circus is this exactly?"

"Why, are they asking?"

"Uh, yeah, some of them."

"Clowns, animals. You know, people bouncing and swinging on stuff. A circus-circus."

"And where is it going to be exactly?"

"Different places. Like here, I think, the Fairfield Junior High Auditorium."

"You're having a circus in an auditorium?"

"I'm not having it. They are. Childcare. They're like the Lions, the Elks Club. Something. Look, buddy, I'm a marketing director. My job is to get you to call those numbers, and you're doing a damn fine job of it too. Why don't you take five, make it ten, go over to the Hess station and get a Coke?" He winked, broadly. The sideburn constricted like a small bird with cramps.

I stood outside, smoking, leaning against the building. The edge of a circle of streetlamp light fuzzed near my high-top. I had gone to the Hess station. It was night now, but still just as hot as ever, which felt unfair. With the hazy moon and the barely blinking stars, it should have been cool out, shouldn't it? I rolled my dewy Coke against my cheek, feeling grubby as a mole. Maybe there was nothing wrong with what I was doing. Maybe there was a Wild Bill Family Circus. Maybe some kid who'd had a genetic bad break would have the time of his life watching people swinging and bouncing on stuff in the Fairfield Junior High Auditorium. For all I knew there was a baby elephant in a baby elephant hat. But one of those women had said that she'd have to cut back on groceries that month; it wasn't a problem, she didn't eat that much anymore at her age. Something felt wrong. So I flicked my cigarette, showering sparks on the deserted city street, and I headed for the Dial Tone. I only had, like, three dollars, but I had a friendly face if it came down to it.

I want to say, right off the bat, that Telesessions was nothing like Childcare. They were on the fifth floor of a building you had to sign in and out of. Their offices were discreetly lit and tastefully decorated in oceany colors. They had a receptionist. The managers, and there seemed to be a few of them, were well-dressed people with fundamentally nice haircuts. Brisk, cheery people who went to the theater regularly, and ran 25Ks for charity on Sunday. But basically, their faces had the lived-in set of people whose jobs were their lives.

Unimpeachable; far better people than I could ever hope to be with my ten-dollar haircut. And what was a 25K anyway?

But those were the managers. The staff, the folks who manned the phones, were the restaurant business all over again. You had to have a certain amount of intelligence and a nice speaking voice to work at Telesessions. But if you had the intelligence and the voice, odds were you could have been a manager instead of working for fifteen bucks an hour — not bad — four hours a night, less than five nights a week. Question: Why weren't you? Answer: You couldn't hold down a day job because you were snakebit. One guy used to be a professional gambler before his nerves got the better of him and so he'd settled into a quiet life of solitaire and sex lines. He lived in Queens. Another guy had started out as a filmmaker, but he hadn't had the stomach for showbiz, so he'd turned to golf, which he played fervently and, from the sound of it, frequently. Actor. Actor. Actor. Composing student. A woman who was hoping to strike it rich — something to do with glass beads. Me.

Perfect.

I strolled in between six and seven. Sometimes I called doctors and said, "Good evening, Dr. Medicine Man, this is Wesley, calling from Telesessions to remind you that your conference will begin in about forty-five minutes. One other thing . . ." I had between fifteen and twenty docs to ring. There was plenty of time for cigarette breaks, and a place to have them, a strange balcony overlooking a whirring fan the size of a studio apartment, the kind of thing Wile E. Coyote regularly fell into.

There was always somebody out there to chat with, but my favorite was Asher. Asher looked unhealthy, yellowish, but he was borderline ordinary by Telesessions standards. He did have a day job. He was a boss in a plant agency. I didn't really understand it. Mostly, he grumbled about the plant job and threatened to quit almost nightly; but occasionally he'd describe some day he'd spent sprucing up, say, the plants of the QE2, which had docked. Asher was an artist. Though I had never been on the QE2, I knew exactly not what it looked like, but what it felt like to be awed by it. He had a pager that he could also check news on, and he always had it set for Entertainment. We'd stand out there, huddled over the square gray glow in his hand, the giant fan blowing our smoke back at us, reading about Madonna's baby Lourdes.

Asher was a riffer. He could do fifteen minutes easy on the baby Lourdes. He'd do a Lourdes voice, then he'd pull whatever fifties sweater he was wearing up around his head (Asher had more fifties sweaters than the entire run of *Happy Days,* in such perfect condition that I would have pushed him off the balcony for one except that it would have gotten shredded in the fan) and do a baby Lourdes fashion show. Before you knew it he had Lourdes singing "I Am Woman" with Helen Reddy at a Boston Pops benefit for sinusitis. You couldn't keep up with him. It was like trying to chase Jesse Owens to return a bead of sweat he'd dropped. I adored Asher, but the one time I'd gone to his apartment, we'd both frozen, somehow startled to be off that balcony, something about work selves and real-life selves — Asher, it turned out, was shy — and after a third silence had clubbed its way into our conversation, I'd guzzled my beer and left. With *Helen Reddy's Greatest Hits*. The next night at work, Asher was up to his usual tricks, pretending to be Asher Spice in his gorgeous Orlon and leather diamond-printed jacket, rapping out a ditty about polishing hibiscus in the Trump Tower.

On other nights I was a tech. Telesessions organized phone conferences for physicians. Say you were Pfizer-What's-Their-Drug, and you wanted to publicize your new attention-deficit-disorder drug. Telesessions would organize conferences with a moderator, a specialist, and the doctors being hawked to. The drug had to have good word of mouth. From the sound of it, most of the M.D.s found it useful, trading anecdotes and info that had nothing to do with the topic. That's where the moderator came in, herding them back. My job was simpler. I hooked them all up from a room that looked like the set of *Plan 9 from Outer Space* — high tech, low budget. Then I listened. If a cardiologist's kid was screaming in the background, I could contact him privately to shut the brat up. Any interference on the line, I was the man.

I said earlier it was a perfect job — easy money, my kind of hours, pack of weirdos — but there was one giant flaw. I was a hypochondriac. In fact, I was a genius of hypochondria, perhaps the greatest of my generation. I could actually develop symptoms as I heard them. I have given myself infantile paralysis, muscular dystrophy, all forms of heart disease and cancer, beriberi, and a disease I returned to over and over like the scene of a crime, AIDS. That's a woefully incomplete list. If I've heard of it, I've had it.

Though I can't remember birthdays, I can remember, with astonishing, laserlike accuracy, my aunt Judy's description, when I was eight, of the signs of lymphoma; and sure enough, when I checked myself out in the bathroom, I had it. It was my first major illness. I walked around my grandmother's for days with a wan, little smile waxed over my lips. I hadn't appreciated these good people enough. How could I not have noticed that shade of green particular to tobacco fields in early August? *Bewitched* with Elizabeth Montgomery, the heady aroma of squash frying, I hadn't even begun to smoke yet — and now I was leaving it all behind. How ineffably sad my tiny little coffin would be. How would my mother ever find the strength to go on? Nights, I wept convulsively into my pillow, falling exhaustedly asleep, only to be tossed back to the surface by nightmares. Finally, I couldn't shoulder the burden all by myself. I told Nanny one night while I was helping her wash the dishes. There she was, in her elbow-length yellow gloves, squinting at a corn-bread pan through the smoke from her thirtieth Pall Mall Gold 100 that day, telling me about one of the many supernatural things that had happened to her during her life. And now I was going to be one of them, my small ghost sitting just out of reach on the edge of her bed or knocking down the rooster-on-burlap picture my aunt Dill had made out of seeds. There was no way it could be the wind. It could only be my restless spirit, released before its time. The plate I was drying with a sunflower dish towel blurred through my tears. Little hiccup of a sob.

"Oh, now, what's all this about?" she said, grabbing me behind the neck like a puppy she might drown. Her yellow glove got suds on my crew cut. "I didn't scare you talking 'bout them caterpillars what ate up the whole tree, did I?"

I shook my head no, wiped snot on the back of my arm.

"What is it then, sugar?"

"I have lymphoma," I blubbered.

She laughed, a smoker's laugh, hacking and honking like gulls caught in a squall. It had a freeze-drying effect on my tears and mucus. "Lord have mercy. You don't no more have the lymphoma than that pot of beans."

"I don't?"

"Goodness gracious no. Now wipe off your face and hand me that pie plate. I never heard such a bunch of mess in all my life. Now, did I ever tell you about the time this fella showed up dressed all in white, couldn't nobody see him but me . . ."

I joke about it, but really, it's only crutch funny. I can't bear to count the hours I've spent on the couch checking and rechecking my pulse, my temperature, that peculiar spot on my leg, how many times I've said, "Does this look funny to you?" The terrible thing about fear is that it's riveting. All the things you'd like to be — a snappy dresser, an astute observer, kind — fade away into the background noise of anything that isn't your imminent death. It's wasteful. People get sick of you. You make yourself so miserable that you contemplate suicide, and then you can't even appreciate the pitiable irony of that. Hypochondria is different from other neurotic fears. A person who's afraid of high places probably isn't going to fall from one. A person who's afraid of snakes can usually avoid them. What the hypochondriac fears, death, is real, and it is going to happen to him. It's only a matter of when; he can't avoid it. The world is saturated in it. Nearly everyone fears dying; but most people make the sanity-saving dodge of simply not contemplating it until the swish of the scythe is blowing the bangs off their forehead. The hypochondriac can't stop contemplating it. Death, its omnipresence, feels as visceral as a black dog growling under the couch, waiting to bite.

Which made Telesessions a bit of a tough break. The first few weeks, anytime I teched, I left work gray faced, my clothes sticking to me like old tape from where I'd sweated through a conference, cooled off smoking by the giant fan with Asher, then sweated through another one. Sometimes there were three or four of these nerve-shredders a night. Conferees casually batted around anecdotes about holes in throats and eyes popping from heads due to high blood pressure and testicles the size of softballs and brains liquefying into strawberry preserves and every other mortification and putrefaction of the flesh — the imaginable, the unimaginable. The other techs hummed, pulled out their nose hairs, had sexual fantasies. We weren't allowed to read. I sat there electrified, white knuckled. My palpitations were the symptom of so many diseases that I couldn't get out of the starting gate of general terror and begin to run the real race of a diagnosis.

But necessity is the great mother, and after a month of limping out of there, shattered, I learned a magic trick: how to listen without hearing. The words became a net of sounds. I could hear when the net ripped, and I could swoop in to mend it; but I never knew what the net was made of. They could have discussed the hour of my own death, and I could have continued to fantasize about that bullet-headed Marine on the subway that evening, the one with the gold chain around the tree stump of his neck and biceps like grapefruit. The train was empty, it was late, no, wait, we'd gotten off at the same stop together, even better, he was a little drunk and he was from Kansas, or Iowa, some corn state where they grew 'em big, I . . .

One Saturday afternoon I came home from the grocery store to find a new John hurtling around the apartment. A Mariah Carey CD was blasting and he had a fresh haircut. He was busily scrubbing down the dishwasher with a Brillo. The dishwasher — a gummy brown — certainly needed it; but then again it didn't work. Pointless? Perhaps. Who was I to say? I raised my eyebrows in greeting — it was impossible to talk above Hurricane Mariah. He nodded ecstatically and swayed to the music. I put away my Shredded Wheat, my turkey product, a fifty-nine-cent box of pasta, a pack of Pepperidge Farm Mint Milano Cookies, and a bottle of Smirnoff. Now that I was working I could splurge on boutique cookies and upscale vodka.

John unbent from the floor and arabesqued into the living room. Mariah's singing suddenly stopped, as if she'd been shot — maybe in a perfect world. I fisted my plastic bag into the spot between the refrigerator and the stove, turned around. John, dazzle marks of exuberance radiating from him, stood leaning in the doorframe, his fingertips iced in pink Brillo soap.

"How are you?" I said, expecting a pleasant answer after the gymnastics I'd just seen.

"I have cancer."

"What? John . . ."

"Lung cancer."

"Oh, my God."

"It's OK."

"It is?"

"I'm taking these shark-cartilage pills and drinking Ensure."

"Really? Is this some kind of new . . . ?"

"Well, my doctor wants me to have chemotherapy, of course, but —" and he crossed his arms with a no-siree shake of the head — "I'm not going to do that."

"Why not?"

A you-big-silly flick of the hand. He leaned in confidentially. "Chemotherapy kills people."

"Uh, I don't know about that, John . . ."

He snorted. "Well I do. I was an oncology nurse."

I felt like I was trying to catch fish with my bare hands. This slippery conversation kept wriggling away, cutting me with its sharp scales. "Well, um, I don't know then." I couldn't exactly say that I was an oncology nurse too and go to the mat with him.

"But they did give me these great antidepressants. And look." He took a deep breath, then blew all of it out. "They drained my lungs."

"Well . . . that's great. It really is. I'm glad you're feeling . . . so much better."

"You wanna have dinner tonight?"

"Uh . . . sure, that would be great."

"What time do you like to eat?" He studied me carefully, like I might lie.

"Whenever."

"Seven all right?"

"Sure."

"Sure?"

"Yeah, absolutely."

"Great."

We stood there, trying to out-smile each other. John had flung open — at least they looked flung — all the windows. You could hear the traffic outside, shuffling up Third Avenue. Car horn. Person yelling. Truck grinding its gears. The kitchen smelled clean. Bananas in a basket squatted on the microwave. I needed to go and sit and think and smoke, work on my own lung cancer. And call Jo Ann. "OK," I said, squeezing by him, "see you at seven."

Jo Ann had very little to offer other than "oh no" and "oh my God." My thoughts exactly. When I told her he'd been an oncology nurse, she made a choking noise, like a chipmunk was scrabbling up her throat. She did ask me what I was going to do.

"I don't know. I mean, what can I do? What should I do? It seems like I should tie him to something and force him to have chemotherapy. But you can't do that, can you?"

"No."

"Maybe a normal person would move. Maybe a normal person would say, 'I'm sorry, but this is none of my business. This is more than I bargained for.'"

"Maybe."

"But I can't do that either. Maybe that would be OK for a normal person, but it wouldn't be OK for me. It seems wrong. He has cancer. Is that crazy?"

"No, it's not crazy."

"Good, because it sort of feels like it's crazy, like I'm not protecting myself or something. You know what I mean?"

"Yeah."

"Fuck." No response. "Fuck, fuck, fuck, fuck, fuck."

"Yeah."

At 6:30 I decided to poke my nose in and pour some of my new uptown vodka. I passed the dining room, which was really just an extension of the living room. The table was set with Southwestern-looking dishes, fanned napkins — a basic catering fold — and two burgundy tapers in brass holders. Tortilla chips and salsa sat on the coffee table. John was in the kitchen in an apron that said something lascivious but was also a pun on food. Mercifully, I forgot it as I read it. Bowls everywhere. He seemed to be just standing there, staring at the boneyard of utensils in the sink.

I said hi and offered him a drink.

"I don't drink," he said, frowning. But then he smiled and said, "But I did get some wine for dinner. I might have some of that. Go in and make yourself comfortable."

Taylor Dane, or some power pop mistress from the eighties, bayed from the stereo. The apartment was so clean it looked like it had been boiled and peeled. I bit a chip, sipped my vodka. I thought about all of the events that had led to me being here. When I was a little boy I used to watch the Tonys with my mother. I'd sit there, exasperated, saying, "Mama, that's Angela Lansbury." I only knew Angela from *Bedknobs and Broomsticks*. I didn't know what *Mame* was. But I knew there were people out there who were not like my family. They got invited to award shows where they wore tuxedos. Of course, you could say that about the Emmys too. But these Tony people were . . . different. The men seemed like . . . they wouldn't know how to fix a lawn mower. And that they wouldn't care either. Burt Lancaster and Kirk Douglas, who I'd just seen on the Academy Awards singing a song with Susan Anton, might have been famous, but they looked like the kind of men who cared mightily about fixing lawn mowers; and if that's how they were going to be, I didn't know why they'd bothered being movie stars in the first place. They may as well have worked the pumps at the Sunoco with the rest of my relatives. I wouldn't end up working the pumps. Men like me wound up assistant manager of the Dollar General. They lived with their mothers. People always talked about how nice they were to their mothers. These men on the Tonys didn't live with their mothers. They probably weren't even nice to them. They lived in New York. It was the kind of shaping thing that made you have to live here.

At about seven, John plopped down catercorner from me on the love seat, sighing, "I've been working my tits off in there."

"You really didn't have to do this," I said, suddenly afraid that I'd done something wrong. Maybe this was one of those situations where the person offers and you were supposed to refuse, or better yet, to do what they'd offered in the first place. I could never get those things right.

"Oh no, it's nice having somebody around again. Alan's never here. He's always got a boyfriend." John rolled his eyes.

"Then why does he stay here?"

"'Cause he's never with one long enough to move in on him. Don't worry, you'll meet him soon enough. He's due to break up any day now." He elongated "due" in the gay manner.

Dinner was tuna noodle casserole and the kind of salad in a faux wooden bowl that a woman in a hairnet might hand you. Radioactively orange dressing. There was nothing Tonys about it, though the casserole was textbook. Mock apple pie for dessert. Mock apple pie, in case you didn't know, is made almost entirely of RITZ crackers, and it succeeds perfectly in mocking apples. If my mother had been there, criticizing us, the picture would have been perfect.

We talked about our childhoods. John's had been the usual collection of traumas. So had mine. He looked nice there under the flickering tapers. The sixteen-by-candlelight effect, my friend Kenneth used to call it. John was hardly old, forty-two or -three; but I could tell that he had been a real cutie about twenty years ago. His face still had the angles of a vanished handsomeness. While we were having after-dinner sips of our wine, which tasted like that Kool-Aid they'd drunk back in Guyana, John pulled a floral cigarette case from the band of his sweatpants and lit a Doral 100. He was smoking. He was smoking and he was flicking the ashes onto his plate, which always made me want to run for cover. But more than that, he was smoking. And he had lung cancer. The words seemed to announce themselves one at a time, as if we'd only just met, which was far from true, particularly as regards Mr. Cancer. He. Was. Smoking. He. Had. Lung cancer.

"I miss this," he said, exhaling deeply, and getting in some smoke rings to boot.

"Smoking?" I said, trying not to sound incredulous.

"Miss it? Honey, I never stopped long enough to miss it. No, I mean this," he said, waving his cigarette in the general direction of life. "Me and Buddy used to do this all the time. Have dinner, sit around, watch TV. Mind you, missy —" hand on hip here — "we had our nights. One night we had about six naked men in and out of here between us."

"Was he, like, your boyfriend?"

"Hardly. Buddy didn't do boyfriends. He did boys, but not boyfriends. Unlike some people I could name who swore when they moved in here they never went out."

"Alan."

"Her. Yes. God, I miss that wild old thing."

"Alan?"

"Oh, pleeeease. Alan — ha! Buddy. You've got to keep up, dear, if you're going to make it here in La Apple Grande, as Buddy used to call it. This was his apartment. We lived here for what? Fifteen, sixteen years."

"He didn't just move, huh?"

"In a way, he did move. Back down to North Carolina. We were both from there, used to rent a car and drive to Charlotte for Christmas. Homos for the holidays. That's why I liked you."

I wasn't keeping up again. So much for La Apple. Tiny smile to conceal blank look.

He wasn't fooled. "Virginia? South? Hello? You're from there. No more Gallo for you, sister."

"So why'd he move back?"

"Well, he didn't have much choice. You see, Buddy, she did like her cocktails. Like you." He said it in a friendly way, like wasn't it nice that Buddy and I had something in common; but it made me want to root out the nearest church basement with an AA meeting. "And one night he was coming home." He crushed his cigarette out near a speck of mushroom. I don't know if he intended it to be dramatic, but it was. "Some bar or other. I was working that night, I remember. Poor Mrs.

Atkins had died. Pancreatic. They never live. I figured out the time later. I was probably just unhooking her when he stepped in front of that cab. Drunk as a lord, as per usual. He never even woke up. He never has woken up. His mother's got him down there in Charlotte, curled up in a fetal ball in a nursing home. She goes there every afternoon and knits and watches her stories. Time of her life. Best thing that ever happened as far as she's concerned. Brought her little Buddy back home. He. Would. Die if he knew it. I . . . went to see him once. Didn't stay five minutes. What was the point? 'Homos for the holidays,' I said. But now he was one all the time."

For my part, I was ready for the suicide pact, if that's what he'd been leading up to. But John, already working on another Doral, just smiled at me, aswim in candlelight. Even the gray tuna casserole looked good under it. The windows were still open, and outside up-and-coming stockbrokers — our neighborhood was chockablock with the once and future frat brothers — hooted out their party-hearty-dudes. Death was something that had happened to their grandmothers and a few gerbils. Usually, I hated them on principle. I'd find myself muttering fuckingsunsuvbitchesentitledlittlewhitepricks; but tonight I felt kindness, or was it longing, or was it envy, toward anyone surfing down the sidewalk on the big kahuna of a few pitchers of beer, trying to scare up trouble with some sex in it. I gave in and lit a Merit myself, thinking, here's to you, Buddy.

"Wanna watch TV?" John asked. "I got the cable turned back on."

"I should probably take care of these dishes."

"Oh no. You're my guest tonight."

"John, I live here."

"But for tonight, you're just like any other guest. And my guests don't do the dishes. *Capiche?*"

"I'd really —"

"*Ca-piche?*"

"Sure, OK, but only for tonight."

"*Meatballs* is on Comedy Central. Then *Caddyshack.* I love that Bill Murray."

"Me too," I half-lied. I actually did like Bill Murray, but I couldn't bring myself to look forward to an evening of his old movies. It seemed like the end of hope.

"And I was kidding about the Gallo. Have as much as you want. That's what I bought it for. Just don't go walking in front of any cabs, mister. I'd hate to think of you curled up down there in Virginia with your mother."

"Me too."

I thought I could imagine what Buddy had been like, rapid-fire, extravagant, like the gay men I'd met back in Richmond when I'd first come out. There were two in particular I had in mind, Dizzy and Rose. Dizzy was six feet tall and weighed about ninety pounds, spaghetti come to life. He was always between jobs. Rose was about as tall, but he weighed about three hundred pounds, and he was black. He was a church organist. They were both from a small town forty-five minutes from Richmond, and they were both effeminate. On the street, they were an effortless spectacle. Dizzy, looking like he'd just come back from a date with Count Dracula. Rose, looking like he could pick his teeth with Dizzy. They didn't do drag exactly — there was really no need to — but they did have a taste for clothes that announced themselves from three hundred paces and anything that reflected light. They were practically the first people I met because they introduced themselves to anyone they didn't know. I was only seventeen, so they took me a bit under their winged sleeves. They spoke almost entirely in gay slang. "Let me go beat this do" literally meant that you needed to comb your hair, but really meant that you needed to run to the bathroom for a piss, a toot, a look around. Sometimes you really *were* going to beat your do. Since gay bars felt like another country to me, it seemed appropriate that this new world should have its own language, though I never used it myself. I didn't have the delivery. Besides, even though I was new to the scene, I could tell that there were little sexual hierarchies; and while I didn't want to be butch exactly — I couldn't have carried that off either — I didn't want to be seen as fem. I had this idea that fem guys didn't get laid. Even then I could see the crippling irony of this. There I was, milling around a gay bar, hoping that people didn't think I looked like a faggot.

One Sunday I was at the beach with my family, I'm not sure why. At that stage of the game — I had six more months before I was legal — I'd practically cut off a finger not to be seen with them in public. Mom must have thrown some sort of cow to get me there. My stepfather, Ken, was splayed out across a lawn chair, reading one of his true-crime magazines. My sister Debbie was trying out her new thirteen-year-old body up on the boardwalk. My brother, Mike, was playing Hot Wheels in the sand. My sister Karen was probably being a pest. She was six. I was deep into character as the ostentatiously bored teenage son, or I might have seen them coming. I could have ducked. As it was I didn't see them until they were waving their arms at me. Dizzy and Rose, headed straight for me and my family. If it had been a sixty foot tentacle lashing up from the ocean floor I could not have been more terrified. Dizzy had squeezed himself into Barbie's pink thong. Rose, in deference to his size, was wearing a tie-dyed caftan. The forty silver bangles on each of his arms were blinding. They made their way across the sand with all the subtlety of mimes walking against a thunderstorm, shrieking and collapsing against each other every time one of them lost his footing, about every other step. Families on blankets stared in gape-mouthed amazement, mine included. I was unbreathing. It felt like all the blood had left my body.

In retrospect, I cannot believe how brave they were. What they were doing was dangerous. It was one thing to lurk in bars, on certain street corners, behind bushes, in bathrooms and dirty bookstores. Sure, sometimes you got your ass kicked by the local rowdies. A couple of times a year there were a few token arrests. Yes, there were murders. But basically it was tolerated. Basically it was right where they wanted us: sectioned off in dark, furtive corners where nobody had to look at us and be sickened by our shameful lives. We were like vampires. Our real selves only came out at night. During the day, we kept those selves tightly packed in coffins. To act as if you had a perfect right to stroll down the beach with all the other moms and pops, yourself unfurled like a banner, was to risk death. No kidding. It was Virginia. It was 1977. It was not done.

At the time, though, I didn't give a fuck about their bravery. All I cared about was that the garlic and the crucifixes were about to be drawn. A stake was about to be driven through my heart.

"Wesley, Wesley," they were singsonging now. My stepfather laid his magazine over his crotch. I could see the rigor mortis of my mother out of the corner of my eye.

Dizzy leaned down and touched his long hands to his knees. "What are you doing here?" he said, highlighting "you" in the gay manner.

"I'm with my family," I pleaded.

"What? Is this your little mother? She's darling. Isn't she darling, Rose?"

"Darling," Rose confirmed, jangling down some bangles that had gotten jammed up around his elbow.

Mom looked straight through them. She had become her sunglasses.

"Well, we don't want to interrupt. Just wanted to say hi. Nice to meet you, Mrs. . . . . Wesley's a wonderful boy."

I could practically see the spears my mother had thrown through their abdomens.

"Bye, now," Dizzy said, tinkling his fingers at me.

"Yeah," I said miserably.

Mom waited until they'd made it back to the surf to grind out, "Who? In the hell? Was that?"

"Uh, I don't know." I'd learned to play dumb a while back. It had gotten me out of a lot of scrapes.

"Well, they certainly seemed to know who you were, mister."

"Uh, yeah, you know, I've seen 'em around and stuff."

"Where would you see them around? You don't see people like that around. You have to look for them."

"They're a couple of goddamned faggots," Ken said. He couldn't believe it.

"You think so?" I said. "I just thought they were like, weird or something."

"Wesley Cullen Gibson," Mom said, dragging out the full armada of my name. Bad sign. "You must think we just dropped here off the turnip truck. You mean to tell me you didn't think they were . . . funny?"

"Well, sure they're funny, but you know, I never thought they were like that."

"Then you're dumber than I ever give you credit for."

"Mom," I said, opting for another route, the high road, "not everybody's mind is in the gutter."

"That's fine if my mind is in the gutter. But if I ever see you with the likes of them again, your ass is gonna be in a sling."

"Who's gonna put it there?" I figured I'd pretty well slipped by this time since we were talking about possible future infractions. Might as well get some licks in.

"I will," Ken said.

"There are laws against child abuse in this state," I said.

"There are laws against homosexuals too," Mom said.

"Thanks, Perry Mason."

She threw the Coppertone bottle at me. "I'd rather you be a murderer than a homosexual."

"Maybe I could start here."

"What?" she said, uncertainly, suspecting she was being set up.

"Get that murder thing going."

"GO TO THE CAR."

"Pleasure," I said. I had no intention of going to the fucking car to sweat my ass off. Standing up, I slipped on my flip-flops. Dizzy and Rose had wandered up from the gay beach about a mile down the road. I knew right where it was, behind the wedding cake of a bingo palace, which for reasons I couldn't explain seemed fitting. Ken had gone back to his mag. He was to a page where a woman in a girdle was inching up a staircase with a luger clutched in her hands. I could've used some more Coppertone, but I wasn't going to give my mother the pleasure of knowing that I needed anything from her. I did pick up my Coke. That, technically, was mine, since I'd opened it, even if it was hot enough to scald the top layer off my tongue.

I hated them. They hated me. At least that meant we were even.

John would have loved Dizzy and Rose. He liked me well enough, but he'd basically decided I was boring. I was certainly no Buddy; and that was only one of the many terrible things about life. There's only one Buddy. When he's gone, he's gone.

One afternoon, as I was padding back down the hall outside John's apartment, I heard these small cries for help. I was wearing a disreputable pair of gym shorts and a T-shirt that was mostly holes, bare feet. My Superman costume was in the dryer back down the hall with the rest of my rags. I paused. Listened intently. Nothing. I'd never had auditory hallucinations before, but they would probably sound like this: faintly definitive enough to unnerve you. No, wait. There it was again.

"Hello?" I called.

And again, a baby bird of a sound.

"Where are you?"

"In here, here, in here . . ."

"I can't tell where that is."

Whimpering.

"Hold on. I'm coming. I just need to figure out where you are. Keep . . . making sounds." It seemed like the apartment next to John's. "Here? Are you in here?" Muffled hysteria. "OK. I'm coming in. I hope this is right."

The door was unlocked and I opened it slowly in case some easily startled tenant with a sawed-off shotgun was on the other side. "In here," he wailed, so at least I was on the right track. About six slow steps to my right was a bathroom the size of my laundry basket with a fat man squeezed into it. By fat, I mean the kind of person who would have to be lowered out of a window in a piano crate when he died. He was also naked, five, six hundred pounds of white flesh, a candle factory after a fire. He was on the toilet, which was invisible under his bulk, and he was gripping a walker. Silent, perfectly shaped tears were catching in the blotchy folds of his face. Shit was dribbling down his thighs. I couldn't believe it, and yet what choice did I have?

"OK," I said. "OK. What's the problem here? Do you need a doctor?"

He shook his head no, tried to catch his breath, snot and tears glazed around his mouth.

"OK. Everything's going to be fine. I'm here now. I want you to calm down and tell me what the problem is."

He shook his head, like, OK, just give me a minute.

Which gave me a second to get a better look at him, not that I wanted one. Wisps of what was left of his red hair rose from his scalp like smoke. His face was freckled. You could have cut the acreage of his pubic hair with a riding mower. His penis was lost in it. Those two rotting eggplants were feet, though you would have been hard-pressed to identify them had they not been attached to his hairless legs. I was also becoming regrettably aware of a smell, like rotten baby food, that was going to be turning my stomach any second now. The bathroom itself was antacid pink. He was garish against it. David Lynch had to be choreographing this from behind the opaque shower curtains.

My new friend sniffled, then said, "I need you to help me get up." His voice was pure graveled Bronx, the kind of voice that usually made snitches beg for their lives. But his milky blue eyes were sorrowful and humiliated and frightened, uncannily expressive, possibly because the rest of him was hopelessly inert.

I don't think I've described myself. I'm about five-seven and weigh in the vicinity of 145 pounds. I'm generally perceived as being on the smallish side. Also, I'm no athlete. I don't run unless chased. I couldn't tell you the last time I lifted something heavier than my own dick. I can't go to the gym because it implies, if it doesn't involve, actual nudity; and I don't even like being naked in front of myself. I console myself with the thought that people who do work out have no inner life. My point? That the idea of me lifting a six-hundred-pound naked man from a toilet was laughable unless there'd been some last-minute changes in the laws of gravity.

"Uh, I'd like to help you, but I don't think I can do that. I mean physically do that. I don't think it's physically possible." I hated to say that because I was essentially saying he was too freakishly fat to be helped. But what else was I going to say? Sorry, I just don't feel like it?

The expressive eyes began to brim again. "You have to," he said. His lips, the only thin thing about him, began to tremble.

"But how? I mean, how?"

He took another breath to still the jagged spasms of grief knifing through him. "OK, see, what I do is I rock, and you put your arms around my neck and pull."

"And that works?"

"Yeah, yeah, all the time." The griefy, Bronxy voice was now gold-threaded in hope.

All the time. Try shoving that into your brain. It wouldn't fit into mine. I looked into his blue eyes, which were now sharp little sapphires of expectation. I tried to breathe through my mouth. If any part of me wondered if this was real, the smell, rotten and sweet, something vultures would circle, overpowered any doubt. My mother used to say, "There's plenty of things I don't want to do either, mister, but I do 'em," and this had to be a dictionary definition of one of those things.

"OK," I said. "OK."

I moved the walker into the hall. I went back in and looked at him, tried to gauge an angle. Why oh why hadn't I listened in geometry?

"OK," he said, "put your arms around my neck."

I did, and he put his around mine. My cheek against his cheek. Him oozing against me through the holes in my T-shirt. He was as improbably soft as risen dough. I'd locked my sinuses shut and took the smallest breaths possible through the slot I'd made of my mouth. His breath was a shell to my ear. We rocked, one, two, three. One. Two. Three. He rasped out the hot zephyrs of the numbers, followed by a huffed-out groan, as he tried to launch himself into my arms. My left foot was anchored behind me and I pulled on "three," trying to get the exact purchase on his back that would finally dislocate him. It was like trying to hug a redwood out of the ground, roots and all. He rocked back and forth like a front-porch glider, but there was no liftoff. After I don't know how many times, we both gave up. I sort of stumbled back, and he sank against the toilet and into despair. In an effort not to pant, I took enormous ballooning breaths. He was basically wiped out, red-faced and dewdropped in sweat. His arms, which were really not long enough for how wide he was, rested on the complicated ledges of his sides, as if he were a chair he was also sitting in. I was sticky where we'd been glued together. Another Kodak moment.

"Well, uh, I guess that isn't working," I said.

"Call Rashid," he growled.

"The doorman?"

"Yeah, yeah, he sends one of the maintenance guys up sometimes. I tip 'em."

"Uh, how do you get to the buzzer when this happens?" Maybe that was none of my business, but if he could get to the buzzer, that meant he was already off the toilet.

"My brother rigged it so it's always on."

"So Rashid's been listening to all this?"

"I guess. I don't know. Sometimes maybe he don't hear me or something."

"OK." I edged past the walker, bent toward the intercom. It was a gloomy little hallway, chocolaty brown with shadows. "Uh, Rashid."

Rashid was a tiny golden-brown man who looked like a trick-or-treater in his gold-braided epaulets. To my knowledge, he had never smiled. He was more of a nodding frowner, a scrutinizer. Every time I walked past him I felt like a shoplifter.

"NO," he barked.

"Uh, I can't lift Mr. . . ."

"McNally," he called from the bathroom.

"Mr. McNally from the toilet."

"We already come two time this week. We're busy."

"What should I do?"

"Call his brother."

"I can't call my brother," Mr. McNally roared. "He's at work."

"We're busy," Rashid said. "Good-bye."

"Hmmm . . . I don't know what to do here."

"Good. Bye."

I guess anything can become ordinary. To Rashid it was just another day when Mr. McNally had gotten stuck on the toilet. Rashid was sick of it; he was busy. Good. Bye. I envied him because I wasn't allowed to be sick of this. I was a first-timer. From the bathroom, attentive silence. I gave in to it.

Mr. McNally sat with the alert posture of someone poised for one more casual abandonment.

"So," I said, smiling grimly in a let's-face-this-thing way, "what are we going to do here?"

His eyes ricocheted with strategies — it must have gone on for a full minute in which my clothes finished drying, then went out of fashion — then his posture drained from him, his eyes dimmed, and he wailed, King Kong tumbling from the Empire State Building, "We have to do it again, we have to do it again, we have to do it again . . ."

"All right, all right," I said, "we'll try it again."

I assumed the position. We both rocked passionately. Think rioters overturning police cars. The one-two-threes

Heimliched past my ear, tailed by grunts that were as palpable as mud balls. His skin was slippery. I heaved and hoed and bobbed and concentrated on keeping my foot cemented to the floor. It felt like sex, the frenzied, repetitive motion, most of me sucked close to pieces of him, the almost alcoholic smell of his sweat mixed up with the shit slickered to his thighs and God knew what else. It felt like the way you learn someone's body with your body. Except in sex, sex like what I'm thinking about, you fade in and fade out of the nothingness of absolute absorption; and here, my awareness of every single second was electric, constellated with whirling stars and dervish saturns. What we were doing was obscenely intimate, something you should never really know about a stranger unless you were going to have an orgasm with him. But somehow the suffering of this poor creature, the years and pounds of it, in my arms, trampolined me out of what was grotesque and into what was human, and that made the stench and the slime of his sweat and even the shit on his thighs bearable.

One of Mr. McNally's grunts stretched into a *whoooaaaa* that fallers-from-high-places emit, arms swiveling, in comic movies. Suddenly he was a meteor headed straight for me, blacking out everything behind him. We lurched backward. If he fell on me, I'd be nothing but a smear on his linoleum. Some cartoon janitor would have to come and peel me from the floor.

You know that brass opening in the doorframe that the doorknob latch fits into? Well, sometimes it has a little lip — I don't know why — and that lip was sunk into my back. It wasn't crippling, but it did hurt. Impaled against the door-frame, too stunned to even wonder what the hell we were going to do next, I stared over the planet of Mr. McNally at the Pepto-Bismol of the walls.

"OK, OK, OK," he panted, still way too close to my ear. I felt like the runt under the pileup of a sleeping litter.

He pushed against the door and got himself sort of upright, dragging me up along with him. I felt like a child hanging from a tree.

"OK." He sighed, a waterfall of relief.

"Do you want me to get the walker?"

"Nah, nah. I can't do that right now. I need you to get me to the bed."

The bed. I had a better idea. Why didn't I just hoist him on my back and scale the Empire State Building? "Where is the bed?"

"In there."

"Is 'in there' far?"

"Nah, nah."

"How exactly are we going to do this?"

"I just hold on to you," he said, like what kind of a bozo question was that.

"And you think that'll work?"

"It'll work," he said, trying, unsuccessfully, not to sound exasperated.

What the hell. I'd gone this far. If he wasn't afraid that I'd drop him, then I guess I wasn't either. It was his hip.

"OK," I said.

He leaned against me, still bracing himself against the door, with the gentle expertise of someone who'd been helped to his bed many, many times before. I thought about that, about someone who was practiced, who had to be practiced, in the art of being taken care of in the most fundamental ways. Simple walking. You'd have to learn exactly how to balance your weight on someone who was about a quarter your size so that one or both of you didn't topple over. You'd have to learn how to pace yourself, how to take these halting, mother-may-I steps, lugging one black/purple foot forward, then the other. It was slow going, but it worked, and he was such an adept that it really wasn't hard for me, though his breathing was labored and his tongue hung un—self-consciously from the side of his mouth. Did he even care about that? I'll never know. I suspect, from our strange inter-lude, that he didn't. He seemed like a person who had left everything behind except some violent will to live, even though everything about him seemed to be conspiring in his own death. I guess I understood that. I smoked, I drank, I ate red meat, I didn't exercise; and I didn't want to die from any of it. I don't think Mr. McNally wanted to either. He was too fiercely expert in all the survivor's tricks: begging, browbeat-ing, bribery.

We finally, finally, finally got to the end of the dusky tunnel that was his hall, there was a light at the end of it, like in the proverb, quite a bit of light, flooding through the windows into his studio apartment. You could see every speck on the walls, which were beige like mine, though age had soured them into a brackish pink that made you think, instantly, of blood. Dr. Phibes would have been right at home. A normal person would have blown his brains out years ago. There were exactly three pieces of furniture — a bed shoved against the wall with sheets so dingy they looked like an optical illusion, the small table beside it cluttered with enough pill bottles to cater a mass suicide, and a TV of indeterminate age, on a wheeled stand that looked like it would collapse if you pointed the remote at it. The TV was all the way on the other side of the room, sitting sentry in front of a closet. There was absolutely nothing else, no pictures, no invalid's magazines, not even, and this seemed strangest of all, a hint of food. No telltale candy wrappers, no take-out cartons, no stray utensils. Nada. There was a lot of empty space, but it was not spacious; it was hollowed out, a place where stewardesses might crash between trips, or tumbleweeds might blow by. Of all the things I'd seen that day, this was the worst: it wasn't life; it was subsistence.

The bed was low enough for him to fall back on, and he did that, with one galumphing exhale of breath. He sat there, looking stunned and wounded, the wisps of his red hair blackened with sweat and matted to his scalp. Now that the crisis was over, his self, the one that didn't need me anymore, seemed to overtake him. His eyes, which hadn't been anything but panicked or pleading or plotting, settled down into the daily business of just looking. They were still pretty and blue, but without the adrenaline glitter. They looked at me and he said, quietly, "Thanks."

"No problem," I lied, grateful to lie because that meant this was over. "You need anything else?"

I was thinking of maybe a wet towel for the shit still stuck to his thighs like clay, but instead he said, "My walker," which I dutifully went back to fetch.

"Anything else?"

"Nah." He seemed exhausted and anxious for me to leave. No problem. "OK, then, Mr. McNally, I hope everything, uh, OK then."

He just closed his eyes and nodded, his version of good-bye.

I'd spent the day in my room smoking and listening to Joni Mitchell and rereading Iris Owen's *After Claude* for about the dozenth time. I didn't even venture out for a snack. Probably, most people would have considered that as a waste of sun-light, but as far as I was concerned, it was the whole point. It was standing in line at the bank and having to run to the store for a lightbulb that seemed wasteful to me. I suppose because it was a certain kind of work that I had never had a filament's worth of interest in.

When I got my first encouraging letter from a magazine about a story I'd written — I was about twenty-one — I called my mother to tell her. Maybe I expected some adult version of her attaching my little drawings to the refrigerator with auto-repair magnets. Forget it. In many ways, Mom is an honest and practical woman, and in her honest and practical way, she said, "I sure hope this writing thing works out for you, because Lord knows how you don't like to work."

Whenever I've told that story to friends, I've always gotten the same reaction: sympathy. Used to nailing their own parents to the therapy cross, they assume it's a featured item in my catalog of grievances; and I always have to explain that no, actually she was right. I didn't like to work, and writing was the manifestation of another little homily she used to haul out — "You work to get out of work" — whenever I dodged (or tried to anyway) whatever slave labor she'd devised for the day. I did work to get out of work. I devised schemes for weaseling out of, say, cutting the grass, which I detested; or else I made brisk, simple tasks intricate — and I don't mean laborious — enough to sponge up enough time to get me out of something else. I could clean the bathroom for an hour. I could have cleaned that bathroom for eight hours if it had meant that I wouldn't have to weed the tomato plants; but at some point it would occur to her that I'd gone missing, and then there'd be a little set-to before I had my ass dragged to the next numbing chore. My dodges only half-worked, but that didn't stop me from trying. Writing was like that. It was work to get out of work. Because real work, where I came from, meant running a cash register for some dickhead who'd "learned everything he needed to know back in kindergarten" — and it showed. It meant either something testosterone-driven, like roofing, or something a little more ovarian, like typing and filing. It meant any sort of death by wages designed to chew you into paste until you lined up for your pacemaker. For the most part, I'd been hugely successful in avoiding real work, and that was partially due to writing.

On this day I'm talking about, though, I wasn't even working to get out of work, and guilt glittered just below the gently
rippling stream of my calm, like some poisonous mica. The
elephant of my novel sat in the middle of the room, not trum-
peting the way elephants might trumpet, but still sitting there,
grooming itself with its trunk, fat and gray and unavoidable.
The other zoo animals of my stories lay sleeping around it,
their paws and noses twitching with dreams. I had considered
shooting the whole lot of them many times in the last year,
just go to law school and bore strangers in bars late at night
with stories of how I used to be a writer. But the sad truth was
that I wasn't cut out to be a lawyer, being the butt of lawyer
jokes and taking the secretary out for a swell lunch on Secretary Appreciation Day and doing whatever else it was that
lawyers did. I lacked some faith in ordinary life that would
have suited me for ordinary life. I was twisty inside, and in the
past year it had dawned on me that I was only happy —
though anyone with a dictionary open to the Hs would never
describe me as that — when I was trying to squeeze the twisti-
ness out of me and onto the page. I was starting to realize
that, like it or not, I was chained to myself like escaped cons
in a thirties movie who were wading upstream to throw the
bloodhounds off the scent; and that the biggest part of myself
was, regrettably, this writing thing, which felt more and more
like an addiction, and less and less like anything as noble as a
vocation or a calling.

At about 4:00 I hopped into the shower, threw on some
Telesessions gear, and enjoyed one last cigarette before I
would be swept downstream and over the Niagara Falls of a

New York rush hour. I was never late. It made me too nervous. So I was probably ambling down the hall when the cartoon anvil of John sitting on the very edge of the couch flattened me. I hadn't seen him in a few days. He was wearing a ratty blue robe I'd never seen before and it dangled around him. His briefs were startlingly white — they looked bleached — and they made his pale, pale skin a white-chocolate color streaked in blue veins. He was classically gaunt, hollows in the cheeks, visible ribs. The flesh of his thighs hung from the bone like flags. The white-brown stubble of his beard completed the picture. He stared glassily ahead as if he were looking miles into the future, and his mouth was wide open. If he'd been lying on his back with his arms crossed over him, I would have shoved a lily in his hands. But he wasn't. Instead, he was breathing. Or trying to. His chest sounded haunted: cobwebbed, full of dust and wraiths. Not a loud noise, but horrible enough at any volume.

"John," I said.

He didn't answer.

"JOHN."

Nothing but that stare.

"I'm calling an ambulance."

That got his attention. It seemed to inject him with the adrenaline that surges through mothers when they stop buses with their bare hands to save their children. His breath returned and he exhaled, "NO."

"John, this is ridiculous. You're suffering."

"NO."

"John, it doesn't have to be this way."

"I'll be fine," he said between gulps. "Ijust needaminute."
And with that, he had no choice but to fiercely refocus on
breathing.

"John," I practically wailed, and now my own throat was
swelling with sadness, and my eyes were pooling helplessly
with the always-too-warm tears; but John vigorously shook
his head no, his jaw set against me, his eyes two determined
black headlights that I was caught in. "I have to go to work,"
I choked out, hoping that the prospect of suffocating, alone,
would slap the shit out of him.

To my despair, he nodded, and flapped both his hands
toward the door.

"JOHN," I said in my best commandant's voice.

He looked at me with pure hatred. I was distracting him
from the one thing he wanted more than he'd ever wanted
anything: to breathe.

"OK," I said. I felt as flat and powerless as a paper doll.
"OK. I have to go to work." And I did have to go. If I called
in forty-five minutes before my shift to say that I wouldn't be
there, it would fuck up the whole night. My boss, Larry, was
a nice guy, but you couldn't put up with losers who didn't
show or were chronically late. It made life hell for everybody.
I'd be fired, and then it'd be back to the old suck-and-swallow
of looking for a job. I'd have to decide between cigarettes or
soup, and cigarettes would win. I'd be buying off-brand
deodorants with names like Smell Guard, and drinking two-
dollar six-packs as tasteless as club soda. Visions of me
behind a shopping cart — littered with a few oil-stained

clothes and dolls missing body parts — would dance in my head nights as I lay saran-wrapped in an insomniac's sweat.

John closed his eyes and nodded again. Please, go. He was begging me.

So I did.

When do you force someone's hand? If anyone's hand had ever needed it, it was John's. But it wasn't as if he didn't know what he was doing. He knew exactly what he wasn't doing. He didn't want to take the one small step that was actually the giant leap of admitting that he might be dying. As long as he was home, there was every possibility that he'd be fine. Going back to the hospital would be the mirror's glare that reflected his own death back at him. He didn't want to look. He couldn't bear it. Who could?

Still.

I zombied my way to work, bandaged in a gloom. The rush-hour crowds knocked by me on the sidewalk, still buzzing from their workdays. I barely registered the crush of the train, rooting around inside myself for the right thing to do. I didn't stop at the deli for the nonfat pretzels and diet Coke that got me through the night. I didn't make sure I had matches in case I found myself above the giant fan alone. I had to keep stopping myself from grinding my teeth into dust.

When I got to the office, Ed said, "You're late."

Ed was the other manager, lower on the pole than Larry, but he could still boss you around and bitch you out and make life hell if he chose to. Tonight he was choosing to. He was a small barrel of a guy with a blunt head and a buzzed haircut that made it look even blunter. He was wily enough to know that if he was going to make it in the workaday world, then he had to at least pretend to play well with others; but at heart he was a bully, and he had all of a bully's capriciousness. You probably know the type. The guy's just walking along, jiggling his nuts through his pocket, when he catches you out of the corner of his eye, and the mere fact of you inspires him to shove your head in a toilet and shake you down for lunch money. There's nothing premeditated about it. It's a change of weather, an act of the devil.

It galled me to be under the yoke of Ed. He should have ended in high school along with class rings on chains and hand jobs in the backseat of your dad's Chevy; but there he was, with one of his trademark smirks locked into his face, and there I was, late. Late, and scooped-out hollow from my latest John run-in; and even though John's predicament and his reaction to it could easily have been anyone's, it felt gay to me in ways I could not define. Even though John didn't have AIDS, my feelings had been shaped by AIDS, by how I was sick to death of death at the age of thirty-six, and how if he were straight there'd have been someone from his family there instead of his puns about homos for the holidays, and even his denial seemed like some analog to some theorem that was gay in its construction and gay in its equations, and I knew that some of what I felt was fair and some of it was absolutely unreasonable, but at that moment I did not care which was which and I hated Ed's guts because when he died I knew it wouldn't be tinctured, not like this, the smug bastard.

But he was right. I was late. "Sorry," I said. "Stuff at home." I knew that wouldn't be the end of it. Once the utensils of torture had been unpacked, they had to be used or they just sat there, glittering at you, winking with promise.

"We all have stuff at home."

Like that poor bitch you're married to. "Yeah, you're right. No excuse. I won't let it happen again."

"You're right you won't let it happen again."

"Yeah. Absolutely. What do you want me to say?"

"I don't want you to say anything. I just don't want it to happen again."

"Like I said, it won't."

"Good, because this is a job, not like some charity you show up to whenever you want."

"I got it."

He thought about that, like a bulldog contemplating a bone. Decided he'd had enough. "OK. As long as we're clear about this. Get to work."

Ed: workplace rampage waiting to happen. Fortunately I wasn't the man to trigger it.

Can I pause here for a word about straight men, or rather, me and straight men? I used to say, jokingly, that I was prejudiced against straight men, and that used to infuriate Mark, my boyfriend at the time. He'd always say, why was it OK for me to go around spouting off, if it wasn't for them? Theoretically I was on his side; but these things don't live in the cool, well-lighted place of theory — they live in the stricken hovel of the heart. Personally I didn't care if straight men liked me or not, as long as they couldn't fire me, kick me out of my own house, or throw me in the slammer.

When I was little, the men and the women of my family were starkly divided. The men stood outside with one foot on the fender of their pickups, passing a whiskey bottle and talking about killing things, animals mostly, and games that involved the throwing or hitting of balls. There were detailed discussions of automobile engines and less detailed discussions of what they'd do if they ran this country, which basically boiled down to more guns, less taxes, and shipping all the malcontents either over to Russia or back where they came from. I was viscerally uninterested. Even as a child they struck me as a pack of gorillas thumping their chests and bellowing impotently at the jungle. Once they were half in the bag, the pronouncements got louder and bolder. If they'd been in a bar, and not out there in the moonlight on my grandmother's scantily grassed front yard, somebody would have gotten his butt kicked.

But I have to tell you that these men loved me. I was just a little boy, and I was their nephew. Blood, at that time anyway, quilted you immutably into my father's family. You were flat-out loved by everyone, and my father had eleven brothers and sisters. It was a lot of love. You were one vine twined with the others into something larger and more verdant and lush than you could ever be on your own. My father's family was this wonderful, continually unfolding event, and you were always a part of it.

But later, when the lady gym teacher at the local community college and her roommate, who taught some equally lesbian subject, bought a house together, they had a cross burned in their yard, and these people, these men, these cousins and uncles, could easily have been the ones who burned it. Yet if anybody touched one towheaded hair on my head, his ass was grass. In my family, I was "different," but I was kin. If I'd been a stranger they'd have turned their pitchforks and torches on me too. It was odd, knowing that you were in love with a group of people who loved you by accident, and with one genetic twist of the dial could have gone the other way, just as passionately; but the love was so enveloping that it blotted out everything except itself — in you, and in them too.

Still, the men were as dull as the dirt they kept one work boot anchored to. To me, anyway. It was the women I was interested in. This was the sixties, the seventies, and my aunts sat around the kitchen in their bouffants and their slacks, sucking down lipsticked cigarette after lipsticked cigarette and picking at slices of chocolate chess pie. Somebody was usually cooking, more iced tea, a pan of biscuits. They might be canning tomatoes or snapping beans. Something. They didn't drink. Somebody had to be sober enough to get their sorry-ass husbands home to bed. In a way, the men seemed little better than children, the way they had to be cared for. Like children, they had to be fed. Like children, they had to be cleaned up after. Like children, they were tolerated. They were men. Who were you kidding?

Unlike my uncles, who were all starry-eyed fantasists (remember what they'd do to this country when they ran it?), my aunts were cold-eyed realists, and they had a fairly low opinion about what could and could not be expected of men. Expectations included bringing home the bacon, mowing the grass, and fixing things, and sometimes the men had to be bullied into these few, simple tasks. My aunts were more than willing to do the bullying. Stamina and a willingness to mix it up were the virtues prized by the women in my father's family. I grew up believing that women were supposed to be tough customers. That was my idea of womanly glamour.

But it was only part of why I hung around, sometimes crawling under the table with their chipped toenail polish and their flip-flops, or leaning against a cabinet by my grand-mother's legs while she stirred one of the pots that always seemed to be on the boil, or cutting for myself another chunk of my aunt Gail's gooey orange slice cake, or squeezing into a chair with one of them, where they'd absently drop an arm around me or rub the bristles of my crew cut as they gobbled down another cigarette and shucked corn and kept some young'un in line and God help him if she had to get up from that table, and in general did the two or three things at once that they were always in the middle of, one of which, always, was talking. Voices percolated like the coffee that forever gurgled on the counter. But unlike the men, poor bastards, whose ramblings always seemed to have numbers in them — points on a buck or points on a scoreboard — the women told stories biblical with drama. Birth. Betrayal. Accidents. Illness. And sex. Sort of.

That talk was hard to decipher, but I understood enough to figure out that there was something ungovernable out there in the dark wilds where the world of women intersected with the world of men. It made marriages and it shattered marriages and it got girls into trouble and sometimes men found themselves looking down the wrong end of a shotgun because of it. Who could get it up for a carburetor when something had happened in a motel and she'd "lost the baby" and Aunt Lois had personally seen the so-and-so up at the Roses buying a locket and don't think she didn't give him a look to let him know exactly what she thought about that especially after his brother like to tore his arm off when the tractor rolled over on him, nothing but jelly in a socket, and you'd think people'd learn from a thing like that, but you couldn't tell nobody nothing, especially not a man, not when it came to that (raised eyebrow here), but just you wait, one day they'd be a'laying there just like poor Beulah, they like to have killt her up there in the hospital, she had knots, they said they were knots, but anybody could see plain as day they were tumors, can't even hardly lift a spoonful of corn pudding to her lips. . . . That's the *Reader's Digest* condensed version, which seemed to be the only books my aunts ever read (my uncles didn't read). A whole hour might be spent on Beulah alone.

Then the next week you'd see Beulah at the feed store, a chicken feather she didn't know was there caught in her home perm, hurling hundred-pound sacks of grain into the back of her dented station wagon. Miraculous recovery. But that was another story. There was always another story, and that's what I was there for. Later, as an adult, I realized that there was no small amount of exaggeration and bragging at work at these gabfests. You heard a lot of, "And don't think I didn't tell her either?" and "I give him a piece of my mind." They were women warriors, wrathful and fully capable of bringing the county down around all our ears with one dirty look. Some of them really did speak their minds, and they were the family troublemakers, always not speaking to somebody. But most of them only spoke their minds in their minds, revising themselves later, when the story was told, into people who weren't to be fucked with, half-believing in their own press. I fully believed in it, every word of it, and I couldn't wait for the day when the pint-size dramas of my own childhood were gallon-jugged, like theirs. I couldn't wait for the day when giving somebody what-for wasn't considered sassing, because all sassing somebody got you was a knock upside the head or a trip to your room. It didn't earn you any respect at all.

So I grew up transfixed by women and flat-back bored by men. I did have guy friends in high school. I smoked dope at Allman Brothers concerts with them. I feigned interest in four-on-the-floors and kung-fu movies. There was very little talk of pussy. It wasn't that they didn't want some, but for the most part they were too clumsy to figure out how to go about getting any, and so it was embarrassing to even bring it up. Fine with me.

There was something humorless in the project of becoming a man. If you laughed too much or used too many big words or didn't walk like there was a stick up your ass (ironic, that) or didn't dance stiff-necked and rigid and only because you had to, or in general showed more than a flicker of emotion over anything, there was every chance that you were a fag. Those are just a fraction of the rules. Boys are constantly under siege. Practically anything could brand you a queer, and "brand" is exactly the right word: it was scalding, scarring. There's something grim afoot whenever two or more boys are gathered, even when they're horsing around. They've always got their scanners out, checking one another out for molecules of homoness. It's exhausting, and it doesn't change all that much when they get older, which is probably why they usually die before women. They've had to spend their entire lives defending the size of their dicks.

Girls were a lot more fun. They got to get weak over Neil Young and have "outfits" and could not only laugh but also giggle and scream and throw their arms around one another. They could read tomes or *Tiger Beat* and nobody gave a good damn. They got to dance their little hearts out. I realize that I'm generalizing wildly here. Girls who played basketball and overweight girls and girls who liked science (which seemed to go hand in hand with wearing stretched-out sweaters and odd shoes) were miserable. You could see it in the straitjacket of their posture and the straight-ahead stares of don't-look-at-me as they raced down the halls between classes. But the girls I'm talking about, the ones I was friends with, wanted to be girls in a classical, Maybellined sense, and they didn't have to beat the crap out of one another to get there. Becoming a woman seemed a lot more lighthearted, at least from where I was standing.

After high school, and up until I was about thirty, I had no straight guy friends. I didn't have to pretend anymore, and I didn't bother. It wasn't even a conscious decision. I was naturally drawn to women, and if they had some dumb guy in their life, I paid no attention to him. Even when boyfriends and husbands were sensitive types who burned incense, I'd find myself drifting. I can't tell you the number of times I've snapped to during some guy's monologue and wondered what the hell we were talking about, before smiling politely and steering the conversation away from him and back to us. Proust scholars, grease monkeys: they were all the same to me. My emotional life usually consisted of one boyfriend mixed with a couple of gay men and two large heaping tablespoons of women.

The only thing that could focus my attention on a straight man was fear. Having grown up with my uncles and cousins, with the potheads back in high school, I had no illusions about them. They were my natural enemy on the food chain. If anybody was going to tie me to a fence and beat me to a bloody pulp, it was going to be a straight man. Their girlfriends might be back in the cheering section, egging them on, but it was the man who had to kill you. It was a fail-safe way of shoring up his battered manhood, of wiping out any trace of cocksucking in himself. I've always thought that if little straight boys were taught that the one surefire, telltale sign of repressed homosexuality was the beating and killing of gay men — and the truth is lurking around that idea somewhere — then gay-bashing would shrivel away within a generation. To be gay is to live, always, with a certain hesitancy, however slight, out there in the world. Even when it only flickers through you, you can't help wondering how the gay thing is going to play itself out with your sister's new husband, in that class you're teaching, at some stupid party. It's born from the understanding that the simple act of walking down the street could be enough to instigate the day of your own death. Some people, even some gay people, think that's melodramatic; but just try walking hand in hand with someone of the same sex through any given city of the world, even New York. If, at the end of no less than fifteen miles, you have not been either harassed or beaten or murdered, I'm willing to concede that I've misjudged straight men. People accuse gay activists of being strident, but all I can say is: Honey, people wanting to kick the shit out of you for no good reason — it will make you strident.

So I may have had a straight-man problem, but it didn't come out of nowhere.

For a while, I lived in what could easily be described as a white slum. The guys in the hood were mostly high school dropouts on the road to a prison sentence in a series of souped-up cars. They knocked up their fourteen-year-old girlfriends and slapped their illegitimate kids around. Generally speaking, they were mean as fucking snakes. They had the kind of swaggering, tattooed glamour that John Waters once described as "everybody looks better under arrest." Quite a few of them hustled. They needed drugs. They knew by some poverty-stricken radar where the fags who would pay them hung out. The rest was simple business math. It was understood that hustling wasn't gay, and the majority of them cut it out by the time they were out of their teens, when most of them had lost their looks anyway.

I lived in this neighborhood, and it was clear that I was gay, but it was understood that you didn't hustle your neighbors because then you were getting your cock sucked by a man way too close to home — the old shitting-where-you-eat-syndrome — besides which I wouldn't have paid anyway. I didn't want to eat where I shit either. It would have been dangerous. These guys basically tolerated me — they usually only killed their own and I kept pretty much to myself — but it was understood that if I happened by on the wrong night when they were drunk and bored and looking to scratch up some action, I'd have the fuck beaten out of me, and that might be just for starters. So I was careful. I'd heard about what happened to people who weren't careful. A few times I'd seen people who weren't careful on the 11:00 news. I wasn't exactly crazy about our little arrangement, but at least we all knew where we stood.

In a way I preferred them to the straight men I'd met before who were supposed to be cool. They never were. There was always this nervousness. Either they had to reassure you that it was, hey, no problemo, all the while making damn sure you knew they weren't that way, or they practically raised their fist in the air to express their solidarity with your kind. Or they asked you "gay" questions, as if each gay person was the world's leading authority on every other gay person. You could say their efforts were better than a sock in the jaw, and they were. You could say that I was being ungenerous, that at least the guy was trying. Granted. But in a way, they irritated me more than your run-of-the-mill homophobes.

The trouble with the guys who were supposed to be cool was that they were insidious. Oh sure, they liked you well enough; except there were those pesky and insulting safari questions about your exotic little tribe. You couldn't really fight it because your opponent allegedly wasn't one. You'd find yourself swinging at air. It was shadowboxing at best. So instead you stood there, feeling peculiar, like your life was some weird artifact that needed examining, and there was some tacit understanding that you were supposed to feel grateful that they'd taken an interest, and in some corner of yourself, you *were* grateful, because at least they weren't kicking your ass. It wasn't humiliating, not exactly — that's too strong a word — but it was some kissing cousin of humiliation, to have to be grateful to someone just because the steel toe of his boot wasn't aimed at your skull. The whole experience, and sometimes it only lasted a few minutes or less, was like a searchlight had been cast on you, not so that others could find you, but so that you could find yourself: hey you, yes, you there, look at yourself, how strange you are. It was isolating, and you couldn't help but wish ill on the person who was stranding you out there. Again.

Case in point. There was this guy I knew in Richmond; and though he had a definite penchant for fucking his graduate students, he was a decent, likable fellow. Richmond is not a large city. Every artist knows every other artist, and in many ways it is as incestuous as a West Virginia holler. The parties were pretty much the same party over and over again, with a different set designer. This guy was a poet, I was a novelist, the rest was the laws of inbreeding: we couldn't help but run into each other. And every time we did, he unfailingly sidled up to me and made some sexual crack about some boy, some more subtle than others. Now, I will admit that I have used "cock" and "suck" in the same sentence if I thought it might make someone squirm who seemed uncomfortable about my being gay to begin with; and I like talking about sex as much as the next guy. But I'm generally conversant with a number of topics, including art, music, literature, my troubled past, my troubled present, yours too, speculations about the lives of others based solely on their appearance or their appearance on *The Charlie Rose Show*. I'm affable that way. And I resented the implication that my head was nothing but a cauldron simmering with hopes and dreams of fellatio. OK, sometimes it was, but I actually spent gobs more time sleeping, reading, and making money, to name only three. In fact, in terms of actual number of hours, I was much more of a smoker than I was a homosexual, and I would have been a lot more pleased to have him mosey over and chat me up about American Spirit versus Merit Ultralight Box. Compared to cigarettes, dicks were more of a hobby.

So I was suspicious when, at one of those parties, I met a straight man named Tom. We were the only two out on the porch, smoking, and I said something about us being a dying breed, and he laughed, which meant that he was intelligent enough to appreciate my jokes, and then it turned out that he was the new writing professor in town, a novelist, and since

I'd just sold my first book, we talked about writing, basically how it sucked. He was from New Jersey, and this was his first real teaching job, and he was excited about being in a community of writers, the way he had been back in graduate school. He missed that. It was one of those instant, genial conversations unstained by any sort of one-upmanship or awkward glitches that have you fabricating an urgent need to hit the bathroom line. I figured he had to be gay. But at some point — I'd gone through several cigarettes and my little plastic cup had been dry for a while — he mentioned his wife, his kids; and I thought, well, that's the end of that.

I assume people know I'm gay. I've got the voice. But some people are willful. So I casually, but not really, brought up my boyfriend, just to be sure, and I waited for the panic to skitter through him and work itself out as the usual reassurances that weren't. Nothing. No mention of some cousin he'd always liked who was too. He didn't drag out the fact that he'd read Genet back in college. He didn't reference public homophobes like Jesse Helms to establish his own sterling political credentials. It wouldn't be too much to say that I was astonished. I still felt that gratitude I spoke of earlier, but this time it was unasked for and unwanted. He was the first straight guy I'd ever met who paid exactly as much attention to my sexuality as I thought it deserved, which was none at all. He could not have cared less. He lit another cigarette and said something about Hoboken. Everything else about me was far more interesting to him, including the fact that I was a junkie-class smoker. I felt seen, not in silhouette, and that's probably all anyone wants, and more than anybody usually gets. For future reference, boys, it's the one true marker of sexual confidence. There's something sweaty and pop-eyed about your average ladies' man. You always feel like he's holding a gun to his own head to get laid. It doesn't exactly seem confident.

That night, when I got home from my run-in with Ed, the apartment was quiet, but it didn't feel like anybody was dead. I somehow had this magical sense that if you were in the apartment with a dead body, you'd know it. Flipping on the harsh kitchen light, I weighed a tuna sandwich against vodka. Vodka won. Back in my room, I cozied up against some pillows and watched *The Robin Byrd Show*. For those of you who don't live in New York, Robin Byrd is a former porn star who hosts a sort of stripper talk show on cable access. Cable access is a form of folk art, and if you don't follow it, I suggest you start immediately. Robin wears a jet-bead bikini that was probably flattering about twenty years ago, and various colors of cowboy boots. Her hair is porn-star blond, halogen bright. She's tanned in a way that reminds you helplessly of white lipstick. Robin asks us to "lie back and get comfortable," and then other, current porn stars strip to the usual titty-bar songs. Afterward, Robin interviews the lot of them. Where they're dancing. Do they have any movies coming out? How long have they been in the business? It's a call-in so some of the home viewers get in on the action. "Hi, Robin, love the show. I have a question for Chad Rock. Does he do private parties?" At the end, Robin lip-synchs to her trademark song, "Baby Let Me Bang Your Box," while miming fellatio, tongue literally in cheek, or licking the nipples of women whose tits are intergalactic. Robin is 250-watt cheerful, a socialite who's thrown a party and worries that if she doesn't laugh every five seconds at the top of her lungs, then the whole thing is going to bomb. About the first fifty or sixty times, *The Robin Byrd Show* is an astonishment. Have sex and banality and commerce and klutzy production values and an insider's smirky knowingness ever been blended together in quite this way? No. Never. It's like a strawberry daiquiri, sweet, too sweet really, and candy colored, but spiked with demon rum. A person with his finger on the button, in the throes of dangerous doubts about the future of civilization, should be cautioned not to watch it. He'd push that button. But I wasn't that person. I watched one of the guest strippers — a man with the angular face of a drug addict and a pimple on his butt — with all the calm assurance of a person with a plan.

Alan was, you may remember, the other spectral roommate. He lived in an eensy room off the kitchen that I had half-glimpsed through the slatted folding doors that just barely kept it private. Nights in the kitchen after work, I'd heard voices behind that door. Sometimes there was evidence of him in the bathroom we shared: a forgotten razor with fleas of hair stuck to it, some lingering cologne-ish scent that made me sneeze. The occasional beer that wasn't mine in the fridge. There was mail John had slung across the dining-room table, mostly fat packs of coupons and address labels from Save the

Children. That's where I got Alan's last name. I also remembered that Alan worked in an office at NYU or Columbia or someplace like that. Anyway, it was remarkably easy to track him down. It required no sleuthing. All I did was call. It took about ten seconds.

"Uh, hi Alan, this is Wesley." Pause as he scraped the barrel of his brain, trying to pin the name to some former fuck. "Your roommate." Still no response. "Your other roommate."

"Oh, Wesley, hi. How you doing, dude? Hey, I've been thinking we need to get together some night, have a drink, you know, get to know each other."

"How about tonight?"

"No can do. I got a date."

"We really need to talk."

"What up?"

"Have you seen John lately?"

"Mmmmmm, no."

"Well, he's dying."

Pause. Sigh. Papers rustling. "Fuck. What do you mean, dying?"

I described John on the couch.

"What do you want me to do about it?" he said.

"I want you to talk to him. I mean, how long have you lived there?"

"Few years."

"He won't listen to me, but maybe he'll listen to you. He needs to be in a hospital. If we don't do something, and I mean now, today, one of us is going to come home to a corpse, soon, and the next day we'll be out of this apartment on our asses."

"Goddamn him."

"Well . . . I don't know . . . but we need to do this. Tonight."

"Do what?"

"Gang up on him."

"Shit. OK. I guess. Tell you what. Meet me at Diamonds at like six."

Diamonds was the kitchenette-size piano bar on our block. It was the only remotely gay place within walking distance. I'd been there a few times, hoping to get laid. I hadn't even come close. There seemed to be only two kinds of men at Diamonds: older men with odd hair that suggested a nasty run-in with a Clairol bottle, or men in their twenties and thirties who wouldn't have made it in the WWF of a real cruise bar because there was something odd about them too. They were wearing either Michael Jackson's old red leather jacket from the "Thriller" video, or pants that seemed Sansabelt, even when they weren't. The place reeked of alcoholism and everyone smoked. Most people drank brown liquor drinks with fruit in them. You overheard conversations about how snobby other bars were.

The waitresses sang between slinging cocktails. "Tomorrow," "New York, New York," "Memory." It was enough to send you rocketing back into the nearest closet. The pianist was always some guy with airbrushed hair who seemed like he should be wearing a dickey. He always had a determined gaiety spiked with disappointment, someone who'd made it out of the backwater but not to Broadway. I'd never been much of a theater queen, but I had my own longings of a literary kind, and as far as I knew, no amusing caricatures of me had ever appeared in the *New York Review of Books,* my Broadway. That was the problem with bars. Everyone's dreams seem to leak and get all over the floor.

So I sat there, nonchalantly swirling my martini, and smoking in a manner that I hoped suggested an otherworldly sensitivity coupled with an earthy sexuality topped off with a dash of piquant wistfulness. It was a lot to ask of a drink and a smoke, and there didn't appear to be any takers. I sneaked peeks of myself in the dim mirror above the glittering forest of the liquor bottles to see how I was faring in this light. Did I have a certain boyish, masculine quality or had I too succumbed to whatever spell had been cast over the men of Diamonds? That was the dilemma, of course. You never really knew. The man a few stools down, with hair like spun Tupperware, a ransom of fat, gold rings on his fingers, and an eerie tan, was clearly doing the best he could. In fact, you could tell from his boutique cashmere sweater that he was really, really trying. But he'd probably have come off a lot better bald, ringless, and human colored. I'd also have exchanged the sweater for a flannel shirt, something smart but casual, but nothing too butch, from the way he conducted with that baton of a Gauloise. He needed something to distract you from the *Sunset Boulevard* associations that were gathering around him like big, black crows.

I was just about to call that Christian group that converts gay people when Alan tapped me on the shoulder and said my name.

He was cute, dark, probably around thirty, with thick, wavy black hair. He looked like he should be picking grapes — shirtless — somewhere off the Mediterranean. In his jean jacket and his sneakers, he'd cornered the market in boyish/masculine. I realized, instantly, that I had one of those shiv-to-the-rib crushes that are never anything but trouble. The only thing I didn't like about him was his bill-of-goods smile.

We shook. He straddled a stool and ordered a beer. We chatted, how nice it was to finally meet. It turned out he was American Indian from somewhere out West. He was a likable enough fellow, but he also had the tinselly charm of somebody who's always on the make. My guardian angel, who at times could be a paranoid nut, told me to put the brakes on the crush. I did my best.

After a couple of drinks I brought up John.

"So," I said, "what do you think we should say?"

"I don't know. This is hard for me. I'm, uh, HIV. My doctor wants me to go on the cocktail, my T cells are like fifty, and my viral load is through the roof, but I don't know. All those drugs. I just don't want to do it." He stared steadily at his Bud, peeling the label.

What do you say to that? I never knew, so I said, "You look great," like he was a guest on my private talk show.

His smile told me that looking great was no consolation prize. "I get night sweats sometimes, and fevers. I'm gonna beat this thing, though. I, uh, this is really bad timing for me. I'm seeing this guy out in Queens. His lover is sick, well, they're not really lovers anymore, but Sal, that's my boyfriend, he feels kind of obligated, you know. I mean they don't have sex anymore or anything, but they do live together . . ."

"So where do you guys . . . meet?"

"At my place, John's."

"But I never see you guys there."

"You never heard us fucking? I'm pretty loud. We're probably asleep by the time you get home. We both get up pretty early. I hear you come in sometimes."

"Sorry."

"I didn't mean it like that." He sighed. "You know, I don't have any place to go if John dies. Sal can't put me up. I don't know. Like I have some friends, but they're not really crash friends. I make a decent living but I don't have the money to get an apartment. The only reason I stay in that room is 'cause it's so cheap. Fucking John, man. Our last roommate moved out because John hadn't been paying the rent or the electricity."

As he spoke, my own prospects twisted into focus. I had very little money myself. I did have crash friends, but you could only camp out on somebody's couch for so long. What in the hell was I going to do?

Back in Richmond, people moved to New York all the time for a change of luck, a fresh start, their big break. Some of them made it, sometimes the most unlikely ones. There was one woman who'd lived down the hall from me when I was in college. She was about six feet of swizzle stick with a cloud of black, curly hair like a curse of bees. Personally I thought she looked weird. But one day, as I was balancing some groceries on my bike and digging for my keys, she dashed down the hall and shrieked, "I'm moving to New York to become a model!" I looked at the too-large features of her face — like the bees of her hair had stung her — and I thought, "Yeah, right after I swing by Oz to be declared First Wizard Deluxe."

"That's great," I said, trying to compensate for my cold disbelief with a huckster's enthusiasm.

"Yeah. Wow." She bent down from the tower of herself, grabbed my shoulders, a big smile on the big lips of her big face. She shook me, or tried to anyway — a cup of nonfat yogurt must have felt like ten dead tons in the mascara wands of her arms — and said, "Wish me luck."

Heartbreaking, and for weeks afterward I told the story of this poor deluded freak and her sad little dream. I guess I don't have to tell you that not three months later I opened *Vogue* magazine to find her in an Avedon photograph eating Austrian chocolate from a Bennis Edwards gold lamé pump. If it hadn't been for the carnival of her hair, I never would have recognized her. She was absurdly pretty. I never saw her picture after that, but I'll tell you what, she didn't move back down the hall.

But there were other movers-to-New-York as well, the majority, and you never saw their pictures in *Vogue*. You saw them back at their old jobs a year or two later, bartending or minding the cash register of some alternative store that sold things to pierce yourself with and interesting T-shirts. When you asked them about the big city, there were vague intimations of hardship, averted eyes, a quick change of subject. Humiliating. One guy I knew had stumbled out of a sex club at some harrowing hour of the morning, his head a jumble of X and K and God only knew what other letters of the drug alphabet; and he'd staggered to Amtrak to hop the next train back to Richmond. He left everything behind, the stack of *HX* on the coffee table, the Kiehl's skin products, the hopes he'd had for a better life. He was now the head waiter at an Applebee's and lived in the den of his parents' suburban bungalow. You saw him occasionally in local productions of this or that, and you'd sit there thinking, this guy should really try to make it in New York. He was that good. But then you'd remember that he already had. For me, he was Cautionary Tale Numero Uno. He was what happened when you moved to New York and failed, Failed, FAILED.

I could of course move to Washington, set myself up in a modest studio decorated with framed postcards I'd bought at the Hirschhorn, get a job behind the cosmetics counter of a pharmacy. A cat. My knitting. A quiet suicide in the tub one Sunday afternoon as I was listening to chamber pieces on NPR. Or San Francisco. I'd lived there for six disastrous months once (a love affair — don't ask). I could . . . what? Set myself up in a modest studio decorated with framed postcards from the San Francisco Museum of Modern Art, get a job behind the . . . No, wait. What about teaching remedial creative writing at a community college in . . . Appalachia.

I'd wander around my trailer, which was perched on the rocky slope of a scrub-littered mountain, my housedress sadly stained from the bourbon that slopped from the side of my tea glass as the night waxed and my balance waned. Sometimes, Rufus, the married janitor down at the college and my Appalachian version of a boyfriend, would bang down the door, the worse for drink, demanding a blow job, blackening one of my eyes. Another one of my "falls" I'd explain to Candace, the born-again secretary of the so-called English Department. Candace, who wore scarves knotted around her neck every day of her life, would Xerox grimly and pray for my immortal soul. She'd seen too many of my falls to be convinced by them anymore.

Meanwhile, back at Diamonds, Alan and I had a bill to pay, jackets to shimmy into, and hard-bitten looks, stony with longing, to ignore. What was it, the end of September? Back-to-school promises of new starts in the cool, breezeless air. The night sky way up there beyond the tops of the buildings, sharp as a paper cut and flung with stars. People out on the streets seemed a tad too exuberant, like they'd all just come from happy hour. I could still taste the handful of bar snacks I'd grabbed on the way out. It was hard to believe that John was back at the apartment, squirreled away in his dying.

But he was, right there on the end of that couch with his standard-issue, straw-stabbed Ensure, watching a block of *Full House* reruns. He was pale as a mushroom, but not even remotely as fleshy. Alan looked at me, nodded grimly, and over we went. I sat down one cushion away from John. Alan took the chair catercorner from him.

"Uh, John," I said, "we need to talk to you." He nodded quickly, grabbed his Ensure, sipping, barely taking his eyes off the TV. "John, we think you need to go to the hospital. Tonight."

He nodded no, vigorously.

Alan exploded. "What the fuck, man? What the fuck do you think you're doing? Fucking look at you. You look like a goddamned corpse. Are you an idiot? Are you? Answer me, and don't just shake your goddamned head."

John's lips slipped from the edge of the straw. "No," he said, primly.

"So are you going to the hospital or what?"

"No."

"So you're just gonna sit here? You're just gonna sit here. Well, that's great, John. You sit here and you fucking die. Is that what you want? Is it? Is it?"

John shook his head no, his cornered eyes blank with panic, the straw back in his mouth.

"Then you're going to the hospital. Now."

John pretended to be absorbed by the antics of those lovable gals.

"Are you listening to me?"

John closed his eyes and nodded.

"Good. So. You need to go. OK. So. Go."

"Not tonight."

"Why not tonight?"

"I just . . . can't." He looked over at me, calmly, sat the Ensure on his knee. "I'll go tomorrow. Promise. I don't like the idea of going there at night. I need to get ready. Then, I can just . . . check in."

"Do you promise?" I said.

"Scout's honor," he said, giving me the Scout sign and grinning. His gums were red as raspberry jelly. His head, for all that it had been sculpted away to its essential planes, looked way too big for his thin, tendony neck, a big baby's head that might wobble.

"OK." Alan slapped his thighs. "I still got a date to hook up with. Are we clear here?"

John did the usual nod. Alan looked over at me, like, I hope you're happy.

I was.

You might ask, with good reason, why I had to live in New York. I can only ask for your trust here. I just did. When I was twenty I made my first trip to New York. I don't remember the exact circumstances anymore, but I had somehow managed to attach myself to my best friend Ralph's boyfriend's college trip and I was sleeping on the floor of their hotel room. That Saturday night, after some hastily eaten Chinese food that it was better not to notice, we went to see *Bent*. I'd never been in a Broadway theater, and I sat there in the red plush of the seats, under gilt fronds arced across the ceiling, not too far (we were in the mezzanine) from a chandelier — swarming with chips of light — that could have crushed about eight people. I was insanely happy, rubbernecking every which way, trying to drink it all in slowly, but then gulping it down, I couldn't help myself, worried that I was spilling it all over the place and wouldn't have any left for later, when I could really savor it.

In front of me sat a woman with plumes of Ozlike green hair. Exhilarating. If you could dye your hair green, you could do anything. Behind me sat two gay men who seemed to be all sharp angles, from the creases of their pants to their born-again noses, and between them sat their fat woman friend in her spangly black dress. One of the angular men leaned over his program toward her and said, "If you don't behave I'm going to make you dye your hair that color when we get home." The wittiest thing I'd ever heard, but more than that, the idea that someone could be casual enough to joke about anything as dazzling as that hair spoke of an Olympian worldliness I hadn't even known you could aspire to. By the time the lights went down and the curtains parted, I'd combusted into glittering particles, like the aftermath of a wand.

Bent starred Richard Gere, and in it, he was naked. I'd only been to the theater once before, and it was a lucky experience. I'd seen the world premiere of Romulus Linney's *Childe Byron* at the Virginia Museum Theater. My English teacher, Mrs. Sally Rand — God bless her — made us go. At one point, a woman of the court, trying unsuccessfully to seduce Byron, says coyly, "Are you worried that I'll kiss and tell?" and Byron says, "No, I worry that you'll fuck and publish." The audience was mostly men who had fallen asleep and the wives who had dragged them there, and about a quarter of them walked out. I was sixteen and I practically drilled through the ceiling from joy. Later, Byron kisses a choirboy right on the mouth. And it was no peck. It was the kind of kiss where your head twists involuntarily because you're trying to burrow your way inside the other person. Rustling of coats, whispered outrage; another quarter of the audience was gone. I was in a state of paralysis. All I could do was ogle that actor and replay that kiss. I was in a pure state of bliss I later learned was called nirvana. It wasn't the sex so much. It was the passion. It was the implication of love. It blew me, and the rest of the blue hairs, wide open. It made the rock concerts I'd been going to seem like the sandbox.

Seeing Richard Gere naked in *Bent* pretty much had the same effect on me. I could see his ivory shoulders, the hairless V of his upper body, the hair dusted up his lean legs. I could see his pubic hair, I could see his balls, I could see his cock. All of it attached to the paranormal beauty of his face. I stopped trying to see him with just my eyes. They were woefully inadequate to the kind of imprint my body was telling me it was imperative that I record. So I tried to see him with my thalamus and my liver and my corpuscles. I think what I wanted was to will him from the stage, down the aisle, up the stairs, and into my lap. It wasn't purely sexual. My wires were too scrambled to form a coherent sexual fantasy. What I wanted was to stroke his preternaturally thick hair and gaze into the galaxies of his eyes before he kissed me like that choirboy. I was trying to make him love me back from the third row of the mezzanine. Or I wanted the audience to rise up as one and acknowledge that I was here and this was happening and that it was momentous. It wasn't just that Richard Gere was naked and I was in the same room to witness it. It was that Richard Gere was naked, and, for that moment in the theater anyway, he was gay, and all these people were watching. In a way, when those rubes had huffed out of the Virginia Museum Theater, dragging their indignation behind them, I'd needed it, because it had confirmed for me that what was happening was as cataclysmic as it had felt inside me, and I wanted something equally as dramatic and external now, to stamp the moment.

Of course that didn't happen. The audience did cheer and hoot and stand, me right along with them, while Richard Gere stood there, bowing in his hastily tied robe, holding hands with David Dukes and the other actors. Getting out of the theater was the usual sperm-to-ovum trial, but I barely registered it. I was in a trance. Life was being shot through the gauze of Richard Gere's publicly naked and publicly gay body. Out on the street I was hopelessly in love with this brave new world. I saw Elliot Gould leaving the theater and I smiled my new idiot's smile at him, and when he smiled back, I wondered if he would marry me now that the whole Barbra thing was ancient history. If there had been a justice of the peace there, I would have married the parking meter with its cyclops eye of a VIOLATION sign, or the watery reflection of the neon on the asphalt, or the pretzel vendor, right there under the striped canopy, with squirt bottles of mustard as our witnesses, even though the pretzel man's apron was dragging his checked pants and Fruit of the Looms down and you could see the hair nesting on his lower back and the indentation where his butt was about to crack its vertical smile. I would have married my friend Ralph, who was standing on the curb, hailing us a cab, or the Poppin' Fresh Doughboy of a Pakistani driver whose name was mostly consonants, more of a pictograph than a word but all the lovelier for it. I tried to say something smart to Ralph and his boyfriend, Kirk, about the play, but it all came out in acid-trip lingo: Wow, like, I don't . . .

I guess we got to the Cookery, our next destination, just in the nick of time. We had reservations for the Alberta Hunter show at 11:00. That's where I finally touched back down to earth, or at least reestablished contact with mission control. Because the Cookery was disappointing. It looked more like a Denny's than the kind of smoky jazz juke joint with shady ladies and way-cool cats in tilted-down fedoras that I'd had in mind. They sat us in a booth. I made a couple of standard-issue cracks about the nonexistent decor just to let the boys know I'd returned to the land of the living. We ordered martinis to restore a semblance of elegance to our lives. Almost immediately a corncob of a woman who looked like she could have sat in the palm of your hand shuffled out, assisted by a man in a tuxedo who turned out to be her pianist. There was also a guy who played the bass. Alberta Hunter was in her seventies, at least, by that time, and she looked every second of it. But her hair was cornrowed into beautiful silver epaulets across her skull, and she was dressed in lots of brightly colored and patterned layers that looked like they might overwhelm her frail body at any moment, like she might just sink and that would be the end of her. Her earrings were like the rhinestone bones of a very large man's hands. They brushed against her shoulders as she made her long way to the spotlight by the piano. She looked just about perfect to me, but I did wonder how this shrunken bird of a woman was going to sing "Amtrak Blues" the way my Alberta Hunter, the one on my records, sang it while I was splayed out across my couch in the dark, drinking more than was good for me. That Alberta Hunter wrapped your blues up in hers and cradled them in the deep grooves of her voice. You might still be unhappy, but her voice somehow tethered your unhappiness to the larger unhappiness of the big, bad world and that made it sublime, made it bearable. It didn't seem so much like the bunched polyester of your own unhappiness anymore.

As it turned out, this Alberta Hunter would practically ruin the other one for me. Hearing the real thing, the intricate cracks, the myriad bits of mica twinkling in the low gravel, the multiple subtleties of a rasp, made my records back home seem like words that had been erased on a chalkboard until you could only just make them out. The amazement of the human voice, traveling everywhere at once in that room, thrumming in all our ears, and opening up small pockets inside of us that had never existed before because her voice had not been there to discover them. I don't know from music, but I could hear her doing things to words that were also musical notes, little drops, a shift here, tiny novas of embroidery, even something that verged on a roar except that it was singing. She could sing funny, she could sing sad, she could sing sexy, she could sing sexy sad. Before it was all over

I felt like she could have sung the theory of relativity if she had wanted to. And her face was like some transcendental form of clay that the fingers of her voice could mold to fit whatever emotion was cascading or trickling or lazy-rivering from her throat. She laughed after every song, even the sad ones, as if she herself could not quite believe what she'd just done, and then she told a little story to set up the next tune. It was all so easy, so effortless, as if we'd all just popped by her house for a cup of coffee. I knew that she did this set, with the same patter, every night of her life. In fact, she'd done it at 9:00 that very night; but it seemed like she had never done it before, and that she would never do it again, that we all just happened to be sitting there when this miracle occurred.

By 1:00 in the morning, it was over; but unlike Cinderella I did not turn back into the boy from the provinces trying to eke out a sophisticated life with a few mice and a pumpkin. New York, the sunken treasure I'd been diving for my whole life, still shimmered inside me. One of those tourist carriages clattered by and I was too green to see it as anything but romantic. The canyons that the buildings made echoed with it. A Fiorucci store glowed prosperously across the street. I'd only seen stores devoted to one person's stuff in movies starring Audrey Hepburn. A burly man eating a hot dog and reading the *Daily News* lumbered by us, right out of a Jimmy Breslin column. I stuffed it in and stuffed it in, gorging myself.

Kirk said he was tired. Ralph said there was no way he was going back to the room, and I certainly wasn't going to fall asleep unless there was an injection involved. They parted amiably enough for boyfriends who didn't want to do the same thing on a Saturday night during their first trip to New York together. Secretly I was glad Kirk was leaving. He was a nice enough guy, but he wasn't as drugged by the city as I was. Ralph, however, looked pretty well zapped by Alberta Hunter, and like me, he wanted more. So he bundled Kirk into a cab and pulled from his coat pocket one of the many guides he'd been picking up all day. It was cold out, but I was too stoned on the city to do much more than notice how picturesque our breath looked clouding out of us. It turned out there was a piano bar right around the corner called something like Ivories. This was before the words "piano bar" would set off firecracker images in my head of broken-down queens slurring out the soundtrack to *Gypsy*. I'd never been to a piano bar, and I instantly conjured up Lauren Bacall on the edge of a Steinway husking out "Love for Sale" while bedizened matrons shared their champagne with sloe-eyed European gigolos. My ideas of decadence, which I craved, were basically furnished with the gimcrackery I'd pilfered from black-and-white movies with stark, elongated shadows.

Who knows what I'd think of Ivories now? Back then it seemed civilized to the tenth power. There was an awful lot of silver and mirrors and white and candlelight, sort of art deco, though the difference between sort of art deco and definitely art deco really didn't exist for me. The people there looked like the kind of people I imagined went to piano bars, sleek couples or quartets, all of whom appeared to be straight. At the time I didn't think of piano bars as havens for stricken musical theater–type gays. I thought only people who lived in penthouses went to them before they dashed home to the brittle but dazzling Stephen Sondheim song of their lives. The pianist was debonair in just the right way, with bloodshot, icy blue eyes that stared out at you from a predator's face that was also haunted by a tenderness he didn't seem to have much use for anymore. As we sat down, he said, "Just in time for the suicide set," and then he proceeded to sing songs about the luxurious rottenness of all love.

Ralph and I could hardly believe our luck. We had a couple more martinis and listened, and each moment seemed even more tuxedoed than the one before it. There I finally was, far, far away from the cars on cinder blocks of my childhood, from the Foghat concerts of my adolescence that I'd never really liked to begin with. I forgot that when I got back to Richmond I'd be running up and down three flights of steps at the pizza joint where I worked, sweating, my mind ricocheting with orders, pouring pitchers of beer and sweeping up pepperoni and stray onions at the end of the night. It seemed like all that had to be over for good. These two lives could not exist in the same universe. It would be like matter and anti-matter. Something would explode.

"OK," Ralph said, "let's find someplace really gay."

We were somewhere around Times Square, and finding someplace really gay turned out to be a little harder than we imagined it would be. I guess we thought we'd just stumble across something. There had to be gay places lying around all over the place, right? It was easily 3:00 in the morning. It was officially cold and we were officially drunk. The streets, at least the streets we were wandering, were deserted, which didn't seem possible. I personally knew that the streets of New York were crammed with passersby come sunrise or starlight.

This was the good old/bad old Times Square, so eventually we did find ourselves huddled over another one of the guides by a newsstand under the pink neon of a peep show, not that we could make heads or tails of where anything was supposed to be. We didn't know the Battery from the Bronx. I was finally ready to wave the flag. I figured I'd had more than my share of fun and the cold was definitely becoming unpleasant. It was time to curl up in my sleeping bag on the floor and wait for my hangover to set in. I was about to say as much to Ralph when this Puerto Rican voice said, "What you guys looking for?" from over our shoulders.

Jorge was not really dressed for the cold. He was wearing tight white jeans, and oddly, the kind of hat guys fish in. He hopped from one scuffed boot to the other, in the manner of cold people, with his hands shoved into his bomber jacket. Not much bigger than me, he had a pockmarked face, and he kept looking from side to side like someone might catch us. He wasn't handsome, but he did look like he'd been in and out of prison, and that made him sexy.

I was about to tell him we were going back to the hotel when Ralph said, "A gay place."

Jorge had "hustler" written all over him, in big block letters; but I didn't really understand about hustlers yet so I couldn't read the writing. He just looked like your average thug to me, and I stood there, waiting for him to mug us now that he knew we were two out-of-town pansies.

Instead he said, "I know a place like that."

"Great," Ralph said, smartly closing his guide and slipping it back inside his coat. We all shook hands and exchanged names. Jorge's hand was calloused and cold and he had the grip of a prizefighter. While he gripped, he stared steadily into my eyes, shaking my hand a lot longer than was necessary. "Wesley," he said. "I never knew a guy named Wesley."

Gulp.

We followed him to a bar not far from where we were. It looked more like a diner, and it could have used a good scrubbing — a long, thin place, fluorescently lit in a way that made everyone look downtrodden, though these characters might have looked downtrodden in the best light. It was just this gaggle of surly looking Hispanic men with bellies whose best days were in the history books. At least one of them was wearing white shoes to match his white belt. They looked like a little convention of uncles. If they were gay, then it was true, we were everywhere.

Jorge ordered us beers in Spanish and Ralph paid. Then we stood there drinking while the uncles stared us down. Jorge continued to shuffle from boot to boot — so it wasn't the cold, it was some restless energy — and asked us questions that he then commented on. "Oh yeah? I never been to Virginia. I hear it's a very nice place." Etc. Polite tourist talk, like he was the chamber of commerce. There was no way to be bored by it because he kept catching my gaze with his and locking them together the way he'd locked my hand into his earlier. He'd undone his bomber jacket. He was wearing a shiny peach disco shirt printed in peacocks and unbuttoned just enough. He could have broken plates against the knotted muscles of his body. If he was tattooed, I was a goner.

I needed to pee. Jorge pointed me to a bathroom that smelled like a litter box where cats also buried their dead. There were splats of things on the walls and oily yellow spots and graffiti that looked like it could only have been carved with a switchblade. Blue deodorizing cakes were slumped into wads of wet toilet paper, bled brown with dead cigarettes, at the bottoms of both the urinals. I was actually too drunk to care.

As I was zipping up, a hand I already recognized as Jorge's — from the menace of its strength — squeezed my shoulder like Spock when he makes villains faint on *Star Trek*. I buttoned up and turned around, smiling, like, you devil, you. He was smiling too. His teeth were crooked and brownish, like water-stained plaster, and I wondered how that could be so brutally sexy, a fist to my gut.

"I think you like me, Wesley from Virginia."

"I think I do too."

"I think you want to take me back to your room."

"I do, but I can't. It's not my room."

He frowned seriously, he really thought he'd had it made, and that's when I finally saw it, when I finally got it. It was not the frown of someone who was disappointed that he wasn't going to get laid. It was the deeper disappointment of someone who'd had a deal fall through. Whatever else he wanted, he wanted a place to flop more than anything, some place out of the cold, a fucking break. And that made him angry.

"So, what? Who are these people? Your mama?"

"No, but there's already like five people sleeping in there."

"What? You can't fit one more?"

"It's not my room. I didn't pay for it."

He smiled again, but it was a fake Rolex of a smile, something you'd sell to the hicks, and he squeezed my shoulder again, hard enough so that it hurt. "Ah, Wesley from Virginia," he said gently. "You shit."

"I'm gonna go check on Ralph," I said, wrenching my shoulder from the steel ball of his fist.

"Hey, you do that. I gotta piss. Unless you wanna watch. I bet you'd like that, huh?" He smiled again, a little more genuinely, and squeezed his crotch. It looked like he had a well-fed guinea pig in there.

"Not here," I said, smiling back in a way that I hoped looked genuinely regretful, because that's how I felt.

Ralph was still standing at the bar, his beer finished, with a look on his face like, well, well, well. "So," he said, "what happened in there?"

"Uh, he wanted to come back to the room with me."

"Kirk would kill us, not to mention Jeff and Richard."

"I realize that."

"Good. Let's go. This isn't what I had in mind. I'm tired."

"Me too," I lied.

127

Jorge came back and stood behind me. Very close. I could feel his warm breath on the back of my head. I could feel his body even though he wasn't touching me. It made me jittery because I wanted him like a fever, but also because that meant he wasn't ready to throw in the towel quite yet. I wanted to turn around and say, look, my hands are tied — and not in the way I wanted them to be — but it took the last few shreds I had left of whatever it was that kept the body functioning just to breathe normally.

"So, Jorge," Ralph said, "it's been so nice to meet you. This is a great place. But we really need to get going."

"What are you talking about, man?" Jorge said. "We just got here. Hey, you're in New York. Live a little."

"We have," Ralph said, karate-chopping away any more discussion. "And now we're ready to go."

"OK," Jorge said, but you could hear that something else was echoing away inside him, like, fuck, fuck, fuck, what am I going to do?

On the street corner, we stopped in front of about the thirtieth John's Original Pizza I'd seen that day. Inside, a gratuitously blond couple in their teens bit into slices of pizza the size of notebook paper. They weren't doing it very well, moustaches of sauce, strings of cheese stretched from their teeth; and they were giggling helplessly about it. Drugs? Probably, but they looked like they should have been waving at us from atop the homecoming float. They looked like the kind of people who would never die, or if they did, they would do it simultaneously and then have matching coffins to boot. They'd die cute.

"Well," Ralph said, turning around to face Jorge, who'd been trailing us. "I think we can make it from here." He was polite, but firm. Ralph was a guidance counselor, good at defusing any situation, and he'd decided that Jorge following us back to the hotel would be pointless, possibly painful, maybe even ugly.

"Oh," Jorge said, like, I get it. "OK." Then he looked me up and down, conspicuously, his jaw set into the appraising half-smile of a retailer who might take the whole lot off your hands, but for a price. "So you want me to go too, Wesley from Virginia?"

"Uh, I, don't, like I said . . ."

"Or you wanna come uptown and play with me?"

"Yeah," leapfrogged from me before I'd really thought it out.

"No," Ralph said.

"Oh, so this your daddy? He tell you what to do?"

"Uh, no." I took a step toward Jorge, tough guy, bully boy, every dark fantasy I'd ever had.

"Absolutely not," Ralph said.

I stopped. Jorge stood there, smiling victoriously. The stoplight clicked behind me. The kids in John's not-so Original Pizza were eating in earnest now. It was, what, 4:00 in the morning, and little-match-girl cold. Was it crazy to go uptown, whatever that meant, with some guy who looked like he'd stepped from a WANTED poster? Sure it was; and that's exactly why I had to do it. I kept going and stopped not two inches from him. His breath smelled of beer and cigarettes and something that was sweet in the wrong way, like the stale

candy old ladies handed out at Halloween. Even that was
sexy. I imagined his mouth filling my mouth with it. Dizzying.
He didn't make one move toward me, taunting me with my
own desire. He just kept smiling, like a kid who might give
you back your homework, but only if you begged.

Ralph turned me around by my shoulder and said, "You
are not going to do this," his inarguable voice. We had an
unspoken deal between us that if one of us was about to do
something the other considered nuts, the other was allowed
to stop him. It had saved both of us from several dicey situations. I sighed. "OK." I turned back around to Jorge.
"Sorry," I said. He was amused by the whole thing. It didn't
seem to matter whether I went or not. He just wanted me to
want him the way he'd wanted something far more essential,
a warm place to catch some shut-eye before another one of
these chasing days began again; and since it was clear that I
did, that seemed to be enough for him.

"Hey, man," he said to Ralph, ignoring me, even stepping
away from me. It was clear who was in charge here. "You got
five bucks on you?"

Ralph hiked up his coat and unsheathed his wallet. He
handed him a twenty, which Jorge took with a look on his
face, like, hey, not bad, considering. He folded it into fourths
and slipped it into his pocket, along with his hand. Nodding
good-bye to Ralph, and not me, like they were the grown-ups,
like they knew the score, he whipped around and started back
down the sidewalk, the way we'd come. He had a confident
bop to his walk and I wondered how that would have trans-

lated into the way he fucked. I knew Ralph was right, but damn.

Ralph looked down at me and said, "You," before he raised his arm at a passing cab.

After that, I was Dracula-bitten. I didn't have any choice, for now, but to try to survive on the bugs and mice that Richmond had to offer; but that was only until I could work my way back to the real human blood, thick with life, of New York.

The next morning, after Alan and I had had the John talk, I woke up inside of a conch shell. It was John trying to breathe and it had taken over the entire apartment. I staggered into some sweatpants and struggled into the straitjacket of a T-shirt and tried to wipe the hollandaise from my eyes. Felt around for my glasses. Pushed down my hair. Like *Women's Wear Daily* was going to be out there.

John was supine on the couch with his hands pushing at his chest, his T-shirt buckling between his fingers.

"Call an ambulance," he gasped. "I'm not gonna make it."

I called 911, something I'd never had to do before. They were surprisingly efficient. On TV all you ever saw were the horror stories. I nudged the coffee table back with my calf and sat on the edge of it. John's face was blistered in sweat, and his mouth was wide open as he tried to drag the air that didn't want to go into his lungs. He was the color of lemon pudding. I stroked his hair, which was harsh and wiry and damp, and said, "Just hold on, they'll be here any minute."

He seemed to relax, a bit. I felt surprisingly calm. I thought nothing. I just stared into his eyes, which bulged with terror and wouldn't leave mine alone. I tried to smile a lying lullaby of a smile that sang a gentle song of everything's going to be all right. Such suffering. I think that stroking the burs of his hair was as much for me as it was for him. I think it gave me this one simple task to concentrate on while my heart broke on another planet galaxies away where it was always night and there was no oxygen. I think it allowed me to sit there in the hideous morning light, listening to his calamitous breath. So I did sit there, one chimp grooming another, dumb to everything else.

Time was funny that morning. Everything was over in an instant, except that it took forever. The buzzer squawked and the ambulance was there. The next thing I knew I was letting them in. One guy was big and hairy. The other was lean and freckled. Like a nursery rhyme. They also looked like ice-cream men in their short-sleeved uniforms, which only served to double the weirdness.

The first thing the burly guy said was, "You HIV?"

John looked at me apologetically, shrugged. I couldn't believe it. He remembered our first interview, when he'd lied. I guess it was some nurse's code, he couldn't lie to them, so he shook his head yes. They snapped on the powdery gloves, rolling them up their arms. Then they taped tubes of oxygen up his nose. Almost instantly he could breathe again. You could see him luxuriating in it, a cat stretching in a shaft of sunlight. His skin faded into skin color. They folded the legs of the gurney down, like an ironing board, and lifted him onto it. Got the sheet up around him. Then they cranked it so that he was sitting upright. It was all so matter-of-fact that it didn't seem real. It was like some Antonioni movie where everything is boring, but also horrible. John was being played by a puppet. I was being played by a part-time receptionist at the neighborhood theater. The ambulance guys were straight from central casting.

"So," the burly guy said to me, "you wanna come?"

I looked at John. He shrugged, which for him was an emphatic yes.

"Let me get my shoes on," I said.

The gurney clattered down the hall. They fitted John into the elevator with a miniscule elderly woman who had some-how managed to fit a pink Chanel suit over her hump. She had a matching purse and her sunglasses were like two black billboards advertising nothing. She stood perfectly still and ignored us, which seemed remarkably poised to me. John actually looked . . . relieved, I guess. The ambulance guys were discussing the best route back to Cabrini. I was cooped up in the tiny wedge of a corner, the elevator buttons to my back. The floors couldn't ding down fast enough.

The lobby of our building was fairly nondescript. Except for the thirty-foot ceilings, it could have been a dentist's wait-ing room: potted palm, couple of couches, magazines on a glass-topped coffee table. A man who wasn't dressed all that differently from me was waiting for our elevator. His tiny dog, which looked like it had been animated in Japan, panted expectantly beside him. The man tried to ignore John, failed, then gave a little involuntary shake of the head to get it out of his system.

The doorman, an acne-scarred, Irish-looking guy I didn't recognize, watched us solemnly. I felt acutely self-conscious, like we were doing something wrong. The sunlight, even under the shade of the awning, was crushing.

I had never been in an ambulance before. There was a little chair for me to sit on. It swiveled. There was John, of course. Beautiful and frightening medical gadgets, built into the walls, gleamed all around us.

They decided on the FDR, going a normal speed with no red light because it wasn't that type of emergency, apparently. It wasn't possible for me to sit there, even for that short ride, and say nothing; and since there didn't seem to be anything to say, I began to crack jokes. Bad jokes, for the most part. I could not stop myself. It was like a case of the hiccups.

"Boy," I said, "some people will do anything for attention."

John smiled, wanly, politely. It did nothing but encourage me.

"I mean, if you wanted a uniformed escort from the building, I'm sure we could have rounded up a couple of guys from the Spike. This is gonna cost a bundle."

"Don't start with me, Mary," John said, a hand puppet's version of a spirited riposte.

"This truck looks like they pieced it together from the old *Lost in Space* set. You know who I see you as on that show?"

He shrugged.

"Judy, the blonde. Remember her?"

He nodded.

"Doing Major West under the control panel."

He smiled again, indulgently, like I was a ten-year-old pretending my mom's broom was a baton.

"I identified with Dr. Smith," I said sadly. "Scheming coward shrieking at the slightest provocation. I did a pretty mean Dr. Smith back in elementary school. I was constantly putting my hand to my back and saying, 'Oh, William, my back is a disaster area.' 'Never fear, Smith is here.' 'Shut up, you tin booby.'"

My Dr. Smith was way out of practice. I sounded like some road-company Eleanor Roosevelt. I could see the burly one, who was driving, eyeing me in the rearview mirror. But that didn't stop me. I was this dog, frantically digging a hole. John never stopped smiling and I never stopped talking, not until we bounced over the speed bumps of Cabrini's driveway.

They wheeled John into one of the examining rooms, lickety-split. In my brain, which was basically a vinyl recliner littered in Twinkie wrappers, I'd expected the nurse to ask us endless insurance questions until I grabbed her by her white collar and said, "Can't you see this man is dying?" which would of course recall her to why she'd entered nursing to begin with, to save lives, not badger people about forms. Instead, I wound up standing there for a few minutes, bewildered, various people in scrubs with clipboards eddying around me, until it occurred to me to sit down in the waiting area, which was about the size of a bathtub. Plastic, school-cafeteria chairs. Magazines like *Popular Mechanics* that I wouldn't have read on a dare. Rags of hospital smells stuffed up my nose. A few seats over sat a woman who looked Samoan and was wearing the kind of polyester that made me feel hot and poor just looking at it. Her face was as expressionless as a brick wall. Something awful had happened, you could tell. It made me so nervous I jumped up and back out of the sliding doors. The instant the fresh morning air hit my lungs, I realized I needed a cigarette. As soon as I lit that, I realized I needed a cup of coffee. I'd brought all my pocket things, IDs, keys, a comb that I'd raked through my hair on the way out of John's. I'd never owned a wallet and I felt weirdly pleased that I'd managed, for once, to be so sensible.

I spent the next hour or so inadvertently overhearing conversations describing procedures I'd rather not have known existed. I tried to use the old Telesessions trick of hearing without listening, but apparently it didn't work without a phone. I tried to ignore everything else too while I was at it. Cabrini's emergency room, and I don't mean this in an actionable way, looked gray and careworn, while it also managed to reek of things in large glass jars pickled in formaldehyde. I smoked on the sidewalk, picked up magazines from the table, frisbeed them back, stared at the floor. It was not busy. The Samoan-seeming woman had slipped out during one of my cigarettes. I finally went back up to the nurse's station.

"Uh, do you know where my friend is, John _____? We brought him here, like . . ."

"Sure. He's right back there." She pointed cheerfully to the room where they'd first taken him.

"Can I . . . go see him?"

"Sure."

Again. No scene.

I poked my head in, then pulled the rest of me in along with it. John was still sitting in his gurney, his head to one side, gazing at the gray wall in front of him. The tubes were still up his nose, but they'd gotten him out of his clothes and into one of those blue paper gowns. He smiled one of his new dreamy smiles at me. The room wasn't much bigger than him on his gurney. There was a shelved metal cabinet beside him scattered with a box of gauze, an empty glass dish, and several pairs of surgical scissors, one splayed open and two in plastic wrappers, like lollipops.

I tried to mirror his smile back at him, minus the dreaminess.

"Has anybody been in to see you yet?"

He nodded.

"When are they gonna get you a room?"

"They're fixing it now," he said, his voice normal, easy, a miracle.

"Good." I stood there, uncomfortably, that smile stretched over my face like panty hose at a bank holdup. I was flat out of jokes. I was flat out of everything. The only thing I had left was standing there, and I didn't feel like I was doing a particularly good job of that. I knew the posture, but I couldn't make it seem natural.

Finally, John said, out of mercy to us both, "You should go. They gave me a shot. I'll probably just fall asleep when I get up to the room."

"Are you sure?"

He nodded, and it was a genuine, compassionate yes that also seemed to be tinged with gratitude. He was becoming the Meryl Streep of nodding.

"OK. I'll call you tomorrow to see if you need anything."

Not even a nod this time, just the thread of a smile, then he closed his eyes.

By the time I hit the street I was maniacally tired. The noonday sun was a big fat bully. I sunk into the back of the cab and muttered my address. The cab driver was listening to a woman singing in Arabic who sounded insane with grief. I wanted to gouge out my eardrums. Back at the building, the doorman I hadn't recognized asked, "How is he?"

"Resting comfortably," I read from a cue card.

Someone had been in the elevator before me, wearing the men's cologne counter at Macy's. It was still so suffocating that I was tempted to charge the bastard with attempted murder. Something was stalking inside me. It followed me into the kitchen and told me to get the vodka from the freezer. I sat down on my bed, drank straight from the bottle. Outside my open window I could distinctly hear a woman laughing, and laughing, and laughing. I stared at my books since there was very little else to stare at in my room. Talk. That's what I needed. To tell someone this. Get it out of me. Then I'd put the vodka back, take a Valium instead, fall into a deep sleep, wake up, shower, treat myself to a nice dinner out. Maybe I'd rent a Nintendo game on the way home. There was a new Super Mario you could waste a lifetime on.

I tried Jo Ann. No go. Machine. Ralph. He was a very sensible person. Former guidance counselor. Good in a crisis.

His boyfriend, David, picked up. David is an almost repulsively energetic person. He makes meals that require fourteen hours of preparation, reupholsters art nouveau couches he finds at the dump, knits summer homes. I could see him there in his shorts. Some dance remix was playing in the background, which meant he was at industrial-cleaning strength, onto some major chore, repaving I-95, regrouting the pyramids. Poor Ralph. He'd essentially sold himself into slavery when he'd gotten together with David.

"Hi, Wesley," David said, fizzing with weekend cheerfulness, "how are you?"

The thing that was stalking pounced. I began to weep, gently at first, thinking that perhaps I could head it off at the pass, that I'd catch my breath and ask to speak to Ralph. That could be tricky because Saturdays were sacred cleaning days, but there was a certain tone I could use with David to let him know I meant business, that I was not going to be thrown over for Ajax and a toilet brush. But the trickle became a stream that was suddenly the ocean I was drowning in. Ugly crying. The coughing up of rags and filth and gnawed bones. Distantly, I could hear David calling, "Ralph, Ralph, pick up the phone, it's Wesley, pick up the phone . . ." And then there was Ralph, variations of "OK, what's wrong, calm down . . ." I kept trying to gulp out, "I'm fine, just give me a minute," but I wasn't fine, and a minute wasn't going to solve anything. Every rotten death I'd ever known stepped up and set down at the table: Parker blowing his brains out when we were still teenagers, cancer chewing Aunt Gail to death before she was forty, my poor boyfriend Peter killed in a car crash before we even got to start college, Janet hemorrhaging from the ovarian cancer that snuck back into her gut. Mark, Karl, Kevin: AIDS, AIDS, AIDS.

AIDS. AIDS. AIDS. AIDS. AIDS. AIDS. AIDS. AIDS. AIDS. AIDS. AIDS. AIDS. AIDS. AIDS. AIDS. AIDS. AIDS. There was a while there, late eighties, early nineties, when it felt like I was standing on a tiny island that was being mown away by the tide. I could hear the water lap, lap, lapping. I could see it everywhere I looked, stretching infinitely in every direction. It was only a matter of time before everything was all swallowed up, and even if it weren't, all that would be left was this one miserable scrap of sand.

Finally, I just couldn't cry anymore, and I got the story out, shreds of it anyway. They listened, murmurings of how sorry they were, of how sad it was, condolences for my rotten luck. Of all the people I could have moved in with in New York . . . Yeah. I had somehow expected Ralph to say something wise or therapeutic. He had, many, many times in the past. But maybe this was a situation beyond wisdom or therapy. Maybe this was just the lunkheaded world, another one of its indifferent kicks to your gut. Maybe you just had to suck this one up.

I thanked them for listening — it couldn't have been easy — and they made noises about if I needed something . . . I didn't bother to say that I had a list about a mile long. They meant if I needed more listening.

One good thing. Now that I'd vomited all that out, I felt like I'd been dropped from a building. For once, sleep was my friend. I didn't have to stalk it, wondering if it'd ever show up. Its embrace was simple and uncomplicated and overwhelming.

I woke up pinpricked around the ankles. They itched with an intensity that I can only describe as preorgasmic except that the orgasm never comes.

I had noticed, a few days before, that the guy I'd slept with had had a similar condition, only worse, and I had mentioned it, and he'd told me that they were mosquito bites from where he'd been swimming at his uncle's lake the weekend before. I wouldn't say that I felt all that reassured — he'd also told me he was HIV positive — but I figured I wasn't going to be sucking his calves, or anything else for that matter, so we dove into bed, one of us with misgivings. It had seemed impolite to tell someone you'd changed your mind about fucking them once they already had their clothes off. Part of that was my southern upbringing — I probably would have apologized to a drive-by shooter for getting in front of his bullet — but another part of it was the misguided notion I'd picked up from AIDS activism that it was politically and morally wrong to ever make a PWA (what an antique phrase that sounds like just three years later) feel self-conscious. Also, I'd had more than a few beers. It had been a while.

Now this. So I called my new paramour, and I told him that unless the mosquitoes from his uncle's lake had decided to buzz down to the city to take in a show and bite the fuck out of me too, then he didn't have mosquito bites.

Bedbugs, he said, quick as a *Jeopardy!* contestant.

Bedbugs. OK. I'd heard of bedbugs. I generally associated them with nineteenth-century slatterns on straw mattresses, but I was willing to consider them for argument's sake. I would agree that they might be bedbugs, and he would agree to go to his doctor, since he'd gotten us into this mess, to make sure they were bedbugs. He would go tomorrow, right? Then I would call again on the off chance that they weren't bedbugs. Absolutely. No problem. His doctor was a swell guy who squeezed him in on the slightest notice.

Bedbugs. I washed everything I had that was made of cloth. I sprayed Lysol disinfectant directly into my own mattress. I called John to see how he was doing. Clipped, distracted reassurances that he didn't need anything between maws of silence until he suddenly said he had to go and hung up before I could even say good-bye. I ran into Alan, who casually mentioned he'd been out blowing some guy in the Rambles after brunch at a gay bar across the park from us. When he didn't bother to ask about John, I told him anyway. He said something along the lines of OK, yeah, well, great before slinking off to his room, where I heard him turn on MTV. I was starting to not like Alan. I was starting to think he had about as much compassion as one of the twigs he broke underfoot at the Rambles.

I called about half a dozen different friends to tell them the latest and most harrowing John installment. Today I could do that without crying, but that didn't mean I didn't want sympathy, advice, some human consensus that someone was suffering and dying and that it was horrible. They all agreed that it was indeed horrible, and then matter-of-factly, to a person, or perhaps more to the point, to a New Yorker, asked if there wasn't any way for me to get my name on the lease, so cold-bloodedly my hand practically froze to the receiver. It was like discovering that all these people you'd trusted were actually members of the Gambino crime family. Most of them, it was also clear, really wished I could be a little more upbeat. This death thing was getting to be a real drag.

Before, during, and after these activities, I scratched. I scratched when I wasn't even thinking about scratching. That night, as I tried to sleep, nature turned up the heat of the itching about ten more burning degrees. It was like being trapped perpetually in that moment just before you sneeze, and then never sneezing.

Next day. Call John for identical twin of the conversation we'd had the day before. Watch TV, avoiding all illness-related shows. Smoke. Do not think about lung cancer. Eat tuna-fish sandwich. At Telesessions, learn how to itch inconspicuously with side of tennis shoe. That night, call for bedbug update.

"So," I said, "what's the verdict?"

"Bedbugs."

"Really? Bedbugs? Your doctor actually said that?"

"Yeah."

"Wow, that's . . . hard to believe. What did he say we should do?"

"He told me to get a new mattress."

"A new mattress?" I said, not wailing, that would be undignified, but not a study in stoic acceptance either. "I can't afford a new mattress."

"Oh, you don't have to get one. Just me."

"But mine are getting worse. They're like up to my thighs now."

"Just wash all your stuff."

"I've already washed all my stuff." Tone slightly under control, but not completely.

"No problem then. The doctor said they'd probably go away in a few days."

"Probably?"

"They have to say probably so you don't sue them. So, you want to get together again? I really had a good time the other night."

Actually, I had too. He'd been big dicked and energetic in bed. He listened to garage rock by bands I'd never heard of, and read James Wilcox novels. He had things like sixty-year-old Armagnac lying casually around his apartment. The back of his neck, sprayed with shavings of gray hair, was cute. I'd liked rubbing it, burrowing my nose there. He'd smelled like France: unfiltered cigarettes and wine in cellars and some sort of sharp soap.

"Uh, sure, me too." Then I added, half as a joke, "Call me when you get a new mattress."

He laughed, and that reassured me. If this were anything to really worry about, he wouldn't be laughing. Would he?

This time I used enough bleach to float an armada. I sprayed the Lysol can into my mattress until it was nothing but a hiss of air. I stood around in a pair of shorts that I planned to burn when I was done with them, not daring to sit on any surface, trying to watch TV. It turned out that watching TV while standing wasn't relaxing. It was annoying. I felt betrayed. I smoked, which also proved to be not as much fun when it wasn't coupled with anything but reaching down to claw your legs. All the bad habits that had added such zest to my life were zapped of their healing powers. My vodka sat barely touched on my bookshelves, taunting me with promises it could no longer keep. It finally occurred to me to call Jo Ann.

"Guess what?" I ground out.

"What?" she said, cautiously. I have to say that of all my friends Jo Ann was the only one who could be relied upon not to imply that you should buck up in the face of death and homelessness.

"I have bedbug bites."

"What?" she repeated, sounding startled.

"Bedbug bites," I said, grimly.

"Hmmmm . . . What do they look like exactly?"

I described them.

"Uh . . . You know, when I came back from France I had something like that. And it turned out to be scabies."

Unbelievable as it may seem for a gay man in his mid-thirties never to have heard of scabies, I hadn't. I'd had the clap, crabs twice, a "nonspecific STD." It wasn't like I was a novice in the field. But scabies was a new one, and the bogeyman of my hypochondria leaped out of the shadows for one of its pummeling embraces.

"Oh God," I said, immediately assuming that this was just the tap on the back of the shoulder that is the invitation to your long, lingering death. Visions of gaunt John with tubes up his nose thwacked the breath out of me. Never mind that Jo Ann seemed to have survived nicely, not even rating her run-in an honorable mention in any of our bitch-a-thons. Mine were different. I'd gotten them from someone who was positive. They'd filled up on his blood and now were gorging on mine. I was dizzy with dread.

"It's nothing," she said quickly, probably guessing that I had already jumped to the edge of the cliff and was now staring into the abyss.

"Nothing like crabs nothing?"

"Like crabs nothing. They give you this medicine and it clears right up."

"Fuck."

"You're fine."

"It's just. I don't know. With John, everything seems even scarier than it usually does, and it already seemed plenty scary before."

"I know."

"Aaacchhh. How are you?"

"Fine," she said unconvincingly.

"You don't sound fine."

"What can I tell you? Life in Ithaca. I watch *COPS*. I smoke. I take a hit off my asthma inhaler. I'm supposed to have a boyfriend but David's always either up in his plane or playing hockey or growing things he has to check on back at the science lab. I have no friends. I can't write. If it wasn't for having to walk my dog, I'd probably hang myself."

"Maybe we could do a Sid and Nancy thing."

"That was a homicide/suicide."

"Same dif."

The next day I made an appointment at the Callen-Lorde Clinic at the Gay Community Center. Bedbugs. Boy, was I thick. I called John, expecting more of the same. Instead, when I went through the motions of asking if he needed anything, he said, "Would you mind bringing the mail by?"

"Sure," I said. I wanted to do something, operating under the theory that doing something would make me feel slightly less bad than doing nothing. It was grim being in the apartment alone. Nothing actually echoed; but it echoed. Some Salvation Army air was already settling around John's crystal wizards and dreamcatchers and posters of science-fiction places, as surely as dust. I felt like I had fallen through the looking glass and into a diorama.

"Anything else?"

"Uh. There's a little suitcase already packed in my room by the bed. If you don't mind."

"No, no, not at all."

"Thanks."

I'd never been in John's room. It was vault dark and vault quiet, with heavy tapestry curtains over the windows. It smelled like dust and blankets. A collection of brass things that looked vaguely Buddhist glinted from his bedside table. A little brigade of what looked like store-bought medicines huddled on the dresser. The creeps I had overrode any curiosity that might be brewing. I snatched the little floral-printed suitcase and stole out without even turning on the light.

John was sitting there, the snaking wands of the tubes still taped up his nose, watching *Sally Jesse Raphael.* The audience was in a lather. The bed beside him was pristinely empty, straitjacketed in perfectly creased folds. Everything smelled chloroformed. The afternoon sun made the room feel like an overexposed Polaroid. John looked OK. He was breathing normally and was flesh colored. When he noticed me he shifted, sitting even more upright.

I held up the suitcase and then sat it beside the bed. I lugged off my pack, where I'd stashed the mail. "How you feeling?" I said, as falsely jolly as a shopping-mall Santa. "You look good."

"Oh, I'm great, great," he said. "They drained like two quarts from my lungs."

That prickled my skin with anxiety, but I stuck with the ho-ho-hos. "Well, that's, good." I unzipped my pack and handed him a heavy stack of mail. I'd only glanced at it, but most of it looked thick and legal, which had made me wonder how long it would be before I came home to the circling vultures of an eviction notice and no electricity. Maybe all those hard-assed New Yorkers were right: I should find out about getting my name on the lease. But how do you nudge that into a conversation with a man in a blue paper gown without seeming like some villain in a cape, twirling your mustachios? Maybe there was no way. Maybe you just brazened it out. Maybe I wasn't a person who could afford decency and ethics anymore. How would I feel, a few months from now, either back in Richmond at my old waiting job or down at the shelter staving off predators? Grim. That's how. Like it was the end of the line. Maybe if I wanted to survive I was going to have to start eating the flesh of the dead in the airplane crash my life was becoming. But I couldn't, not today anyway, not with the wastes of John staring me down.

John sprinted through the mail, saying, "Um-hm, um-hm, um-hm . . ." over every envelope, like it was just as he'd suspected.

I stood there, a picture of nonchalance, finally looking out the window for something to do with my eyes, and then studying the view like it was Central Park from the top of the Plaza, instead of the tarred tops of a few buildings.

"You wouldn't believe what happened on *The Price Is Right* today," John said out of nowhere. "This idiot from Detroit accidentally bid enough to get herself up on stage. Then she couldn't even win the first prize in the clock game. I'm sorry, but they should just send people like that home. Stop the game and call out the hook. It made me so mad when she won on the wheel. Life is so fucking unfair."

John clearly expected some outraged response, so I said, "That's terrible," knowing it sounded feeble compared to his outburst.

"It was. I called my sister today. She's coming next week when I get home from the hospital."

His sister? The one who'd left about fifty unanswered messages on his machine? When he got home from the hospital? "That's great," I said. "About your sister. And about the hospital too. So, you're, OK?"

"I'm fine," he said, looking at me, quizzically, like would some nurse's aide come and corral me back to the psycho ward I'd wandered away from. Not wanting to contradict him, I tried not to look at the three IV bags dripping into his arm. It wasn't easy.

"Good," I said. "You look better."

"Yeah, I'll be home this weekend," he said brightly. "Guess who was on *Rosie O'Donnell* this morning?"

"The shah of Iran." I couldn't help it.

He made a dismissive, motoring noise with his lips and said, "No, silly. Alec Baldwin." He waited for some reaction.

"Oh. I, really, like him."

"Like him?" John said. "Hello? Nurse? Could you check his pulse, please? No. What you meant to say was that you are prepared to die for him."

"Yeah. He's cute."

"Cute?" Same tone. "Honey, bunnies are cute. Alec Baldwin is the superstud of the entire universe. Got it?"

"Got it."

"Cute. Oh, brother. My friends Brian and Cissy are coming by tonight."

Friends. John had friends. This was a banner headline. If he had friends, real friends, then they'd be stopping by to check on him. They'd be hauling stacks of magazines over to the house, Tupperware bowls of homemade soups. They'd stop me in the hall and discreetly ask me how he was really doing. There'd be someone to tell how he was really doing. There'd be somebody with the real authority of accumulated affection to bully him back into the hospital if he needed it. It sounded like we were turning a corner here.

"That's great, John."

"You know, some movies really get my goat."

"Me too." I didn't know what that had to do with anything, but it was easy enough to agree with.

"I just don't know why they have to make some of them."

"They're bored."

"There was this movie on today. It just, well, they just go out of their way to make people feel bad, that's all. Why would anybody want to go and do that?"

"They're sadists."

"Without the poppers. Listen, would you mind going to get me some fried chicken from the Colonel? There's one a couple of streets up. I noticed on the way down from the . . . on the way down."

"Sure."

"Hospital food. I didn't mind it so much when I was the nurse. There's some money in my suitcase."

"My treat."

"No way, mister."

"Your money's no good here. You made me dinner that night."

"Well, don't think this is going to get you out of making me dinner when I get back home."

"Yeesh, you're demanding."

He laughed out loud. He loved that, the idea that he was demanding, some high-octane diva throwing her weight around on the set.

I found the KFC right where John said it would be, and it seemed weird, that he'd noticed from the ambulance, that he'd then made a mental note. It was 4:00, postlunch, predinner, deserted. Three teenagers who were different shades of brown sat around in their paper caps. One, a heavy guy with a sweet face, was scraping at a spot on the table. Another, a twig-thin girl with hair that looked like it had been designed by M. C. Escher, had her arms crossed like, don't-fuck-with-me, ever. Finally, there was a girl twisting her high school ring while she glared at it. I decided that she was the smart one who was going to be a U.S. senator, but had parents who insisted that a job at KFC built character. It was clear, from her bitter smile, that she'd never forgive them.

The choices were overwhelming. 2 pc. 3 pc. Breast pk. Extracrispy. The Colonel's Original Recipe. There were about nine different sides. You got two. An exact calculation of possible combinations was something an MIT grad student might consider for a grant proposal. I wanted to do the right thing here. After several minutes of agonizing, I decided to go traditional. Breast and drumstick. Original Recipe. Mashed potatoes and coleslaw.

"Um, hi there, excuse me. Could you, so, I guess I'm ready to order."

They looked up at me as one. Bland contempt. The boy, who had switched to sawing the edge of the table with a white plastic knife, said, "What you want?"

I told him, with the sort of winning smile they regularly featured in their commercials. It had suddenly become vitally important that they like me, that later, when they remember me, they call me that nice guy with the great smile who'd made all their days. Sometimes it hit me, this completely irrational desire to have strangers adore me. I've stood in line at Tower Records, sick with worry that the cashier would think the CDs I'd selected were out-of-date, whack.

The boy sighed gigantically. His chair, as he pushed it back, screamed bloody murder against the floor. I guessed that meant he hated me, that we'd gotten off on the wrong foot. I was disappointed, but I never actually expected people who made five bucks an hour to be but so polite, particularly when they were required to wear a red-striped shirt that Bozo would have scorned.

There's something dispiriting about an empty fast-food joint. The flat and shiny colors of everything plastic, the brightly lit signs clamoring with deals, the taffy of old Beatles songs stringing the air. You feel the grease. You see the french fry that the broom missed crushed into the grout of the pseudotile. This is the best we could do? This? All the wizardry of the human mind and this is it? Ticket, please. One-way passage to the planet where the people had made something of themselves. I didn't want John to want anything from here. I wanted him to want something finer, something celloed and tangerined and timeless.

But he didn't. His order came. I forked over the five or so bucks. The girls at the table were speaking in low, serious voices. I have to admit, the bag did smell good. The boy with the no-longer-sweet face clattered my change on the counter.

As I entered John's room I held up the bag, shaking it enticingly. He was beside himself. So this was what one of his real smiles looked like. Every other one he'd ever used seemed like a lie. He swept the box out from the bag, examined it greedily. Halted. "Oh, I should have told you. I don't really like the breast."

"Sorry. Do you want me to go back?"

He thought about it. "Nah. I'm not going to eat this now anyway. I'm saving it for later."

"You sure?"

"Don't worry about it," he said, tinkling bells of disappointment. The first thing he'd wanted in God knew how long.

"I really wouldn't mind." I would have minded, of course, but not as much as having failed at what felt like one of those last-meal requests.

"If I really want something, I'll get Brian and Cissy to go later."

"OK."

He picked up a supermarket circular, part of his mail, and began to read it. I mean read it. The way you would read a German philosophical treatise. I glanced at the TV strapped to the ceiling. *Jenny Jones.* An implant show. The box of chicken sat open on the bedside table, like the socks your aunt used to give you for Christmas. I'd bring flowers next time. It wasn't just a florist conspiracy. Hospital rooms needed flowers to shatter their sterility. When I looked back at the end of the bed, I was startled to see a doctor standing there, an Indian-looking man with a thick, three-finger moustache. De rigueur white coat.

"John," he said.

John continued to read the circular. He seemed to be staring at a tinned ham that was on sale for $6.99. If you were a card member.

"John," the doctor said more firmly.

John looked up, looked down, whipped to the next page of the circular. Six-packs of Coke were going for ninety-nine cents a pop. Cheap. I waited for the doctor to try another tack. A man used to balancing the scales of life and death had to have reserves of doctor's savvy that would force a person reading a supermarket circular to pay attention to him. But he just stood there, impassive, treelike even, staring at John. Was that what they taught them back there in the medical school?

"John, we need to start the chemo. Today."

John continued to read the circular with bug-eyed avidity.

"John, if you don't start the chemo today I can't be responsible for what will happen."

John, feigning absorption with all the subtlety of a silent-film star. Me, breathing like he was a deer I might startle. The doctor, not a trickle of emotion on his face.

"John, if you're refusing the chemo I'm going to need you to sign a waiver."

John decided it was time to turn the page. Or maybe he really was just gonzo enough to actually be reading about a price-slasher on Clorox bleach. Limit, four per customer. I tried to imagine buying four one-gallon jugs of Clorox. Lugging them home. Finding a place for them under the sink with the paper plates left over from a party, the roach motels, the things bought once and forgotten, like Twinkle silver polish for that one silver thing you found in a thrift store once and vowed not to let tarnish. Or maybe your mother gave it to you when she still believed you might turn out to be a person who could actually keep nice things. But I couldn't imagine it. This, clearly, was a sale for people who had storage space and some requisite faith in a well-ordered world where stocking up on bleach just made good common sense. It was a sale for suburbanites. It was not a sale for New Yorkers. They couldn't afford to waste space stockpiling bleach.

"John, do you hear me?"

John leaned into the circular, like he'd gotten to the foot-notes.

"JOHN, DO YOU UNDERSTAND ME?"

John nodded. It was more like a tremor. The doctor stood there for several more seconds, contemplating him. Then he looked over at me with his somber eyes, black as oil, but beautiful, like the rainbows you sometimes saw in oil might suddenly surface there. I lifted my shoulders and eyebrows in a slight shrug that I hoped wouldn't be perceptible to John. Then suddenly, as if some beeper had gone off in his head, the doctor about-faced and left with the long, quick strides of a busy man, the necklace of his stethoscope tapping at his sternum.

Issuing from the TV, some talk-to-the-hand, I'm-all-that blather rising up from the many-headed monster of a studio audience bearing witness to some sordid family they'd scraped from the bottom of a trailer park. I didn't even look up. The odor of Colonel Sanders's famous Original Recipe was lacing itself into the hospital fumes and inventing something that smelled like southern-fried formaldehyde. I thought about those poor mashed potatoes, congealing in their plastic cup. I was about to say something along the lines of "John, are you sure about this," when he cut me off, folding the circular and slinging it on top of his other mail, then yawning dramatically, stretching out the sticks of his arms, which were sunsetted in bruises where the IVs were stuck.

"Boy," he said with one showgirl of a smile, "I'm beat."

"Uh . . ."

"Beat. I need to take a little nap."

"John . . ."

"Beat."

I got it. Nodded. Put on my coat. Hefted on the backpack. He dimmed the smile about fifty watts. He did look tired. He looked worse than tired. His eyelids shuttered down, down, down, then fluttered with sleep. That, you couldn't fake.

In my twenties, I was the kind of hypochondriac who was the bane of my doctor's professional life. He actually took to calling and suggesting that I not keep what were becoming weekly appointments. When he could convince me to cancel, I promptly made an appointment with whatever specialist I deemed appropriate for that week's illness. I would have broken the back of an HMO, but there were no HMOs. One of these men, a neurologist, wrote my name across my arm with his finger, as if I were an Etch-A-Sketch, and told me that he could perform that seemingly magical feat because I'd shredded my nerves with worry. He then gave me a grave look and the name of a reputable psychiatrist.

In my thirties, I became the kind of hypochondriac who never went to the doctor. Thanks to AIDS, death was no longer a sport and a pastime. It was everywhere I looked. I decided I didn't want to know. It was this 5.0 version hypochondriac who found himself at Callen-Lorde, which turned out to be a strangely comforting place. It had all the clichés of a waiting room — table with magazines, potted palm — but it seemed to be manned almost exclusively by volunteers. There were lesbians with political-statement haircuts; and then there were the mostly plump gay men ambling around with clipboards who seemed more like homeroom monitors than scary medical types with the power to pronounce the moment of your death. Everyone had aced reassuring-smile school. It felt homemade, no more threatening than a mason jar of your granny's pickled green tomatoes. I filled out a form and was pleased to discover that I wasn't checking off any symptoms. I'd gotten there early so I was shown, almost immediately, back into a cheerfully lit room that was surprisingly short on decoration, considering. I hopped up on the paper-lined examining table. My examiner was one of the plump men, an eager red-haired guy who had probably been on the yearbook committee.

"So," he said in his no-problem-is-too-small manner, "what do we have here?"

"Oh," I said, chuckling, "it's nothing. Just a little case of scabies." This was a favored tactic of mine. Once I got to the doctor, I essentially wanted them to tell me that nothing, or nothing serious, was wrong. So I guided and cajoled them toward that conclusion.

His smile tightened. "And what makes you think it's scabies?"

I didn't like that, because the implication was that I, a mere layman, might not realize that I was actually terminal. He hadn't read the game plan. "The symptoms," I said flatly, my voice edged by the threat that if he did diagnose something more serious then I was taking him out with me.

That softened him up, a little. "Well, let's see what we have here."

I rolled up my pants to the knee. My pink-spotted legs were something out of Dr. Seuss. He looked intently. Grimaced. "I don't think that's scabies."

My heart began the fifty-yard dash and it didn't care if I tagged along or not. I suddenly realized that the formerly cheerful light was more from the vee-haff-vays-of-making-you-tawk school. I shifted in an attempt to regain my balance and the paper crackled ominously under me. I knew, from *Marcus Welby, M.D.*, that in the next scene I'd be sitting in an oak-paneled office signing a living will. "Why?" I asked, the word a razor to his throat.

This time he wasn't intimidated. "It doesn't look like scabies." He looked at me dead-on in a let's-face-this-thing way.

I wasn't facing anything without a fight. "It looks exactly like scabies. I looked it up on the Internet." Which was the God's honest truth. A friend who believed that the Internet was Canaan (if Canaan had been crossed with Sodom and Gomorrah) had convinced me to pop by for a look-see. Which I had. And my symptoms had been classic. Textbook. Any fool could have diagnosed it. Except this one. "I'm just here for the medicine."

"I don't know about that," he said, making a skeptical face in case I was the kind of person who needed his conversations illustrated.

I took a deep breath to mix the helium filling my head with some stabilizing oxygen. "What do you think it might be?" As I waited for him to say the A-word, something porcupine quilled tingled in the tar of my chest.

"Tertiary syphilis."

"What?"

"Tertiary syphilis."

I knew, from biographies of French symbolist poets, what "tertiary syphilis" meant. It meant blindness, a diaper, barking at your own shadow in a madhouse. Death was the final prize. I also knew, for a fact, that I didn't have tertiary syphilis because you didn't catch tertiary syphilis from anybody. You developed it after years of first- and second-stage syphilis. And I had definitely caught this from a certain person whose neck I intended to wring like a barnyard chicken's as soon as I stomped out of here. "This is not tertiary syphilis."

"Well, I'd like you to have a blood test."

I'm sorry, but I was not the kind of person who could show up for a simple tube of salve and have some evil queen wave a wand over it, abracadabra, and turn it into a needle in my vein. I had to work up to that. "I don't want a blood test," I ground out.

He considered me with the same disappointed little expression that you might use on a child in a high chair who could not keep the strained string beans from bubbling up out of his mouth. "It won't take more than a few seconds."

"I don't need a blood test."

"I think you do." He tried a tiny, tentative smile on me.

"I. Do not. Have. Tertiary syphilis. You don't. Catch. Tertiary syphilis from somebody."

"All right." He put his PaperMate behind his ear and let the clipboard drop to his side. He'd had it. Clearly he had a brat on his hands here who was determined to flout medical convention. "I'd like the doctor on duty to have a look at you."

I sighed. "All right."

"Follow me," he said, like: It's your funeral.

I hustled the backpack over my shoulder and trailed him through a warren of cubicles that made the place look like some fly-by-night real estate scam. He pointed to another room, identical to the one we'd just vacated, and said, without stopping, "In there," in his best prison-matron-before-the-frisk voice.

I hopped up on the twin sister of the other examining table. Same crackling paper. I was frantic. OK it wasn't syphilis I knew that but maybe it wasn't scabies fucking Internet it was AIDS damn damn damn why had I slept with that fucking guy I knew he was fucking positive I mean fuck I mean fuck fuck all that stupid literature about safe sex ha great God I didn't want to die not like that the way I knew you died and all the time before the coughs that turned out to be nothing until they turned out to be some hideous thing only Southeast Asian monkeys used to get like my poor friend Kevin dying and dying and dying and I was not a person I was not who could suffer who was but I really wasn't I knew myself I almost fainted the first time I found out I was negative literally had to put my head between my legs fuck fuck fuck I didn't want to die my family'd be horrible already weird enough about me being gay and my mother could not deal with illness could not the embarrassment first I'd lived gay and now I'd die it too like an affront like I'd planned it that way I'd be fucking dying and they'd be fucking embarrassed I wouldn't die at home wouldn't couldn't my friends would just have to take care of me there I'd be dying on somebody's couch . . .

"Wesley?"

It was the death squad, that orderly or candy striper or whatever the hell he was with his arms crossed over the clipboard held to his know-it-all chest, and a real doctor, in real doctor drag, with salt-and-pepper, daytime-TV hair. Under almost any other circumstances I would have found him so threateningly handsome I couldn't have even fantasized about him; but tonight my head was nothing but clusters of soap bubbles glassy with fantasies of my own death.

"Yeah?"

"Let's have a look here," the doctor said, almost jolly.

I dutifully re–rolled up my pants. He stared. I stared. We all stared.

He looked up at me. Kindly smile that crinkled his eyes. "You know what? I think you should have a blood test."

If my muscles hadn't been watery with fear I would have leaped from the table to savagely slap the I-told-you-sos from Candy Striper's face. "Why?" I barely got it out.

"Just a little precaution."

"Against what?" My voice quavered like Katharine Hepburn's in one of her later movies. I waited for him to say. It.

"It might be tertiary syphilis."

Tertiary syphilis? Were we back to that? What about AIDS? What about the cockhead I'd slept with who was the reason I was here in the first place? What about not having any damned health insurance so I had to go to places like this to begin with? What about this stupid fucking world where everyone seemed to be dying? What about scaring the shit out of somebody because you couldn't make a simple diagnosis of scabies? My terror wobbled over into anger and that was getting caught up in the concentric circles of relief that he hadn't said AIDS. Tertiary syphilis? What medical school in the Caribbean had he graduated from?

"This is not tertiary syphilis. You don't catch tertiary syphilis from someone. Do you?"

"That's true." He was trying to be reasonable. I could see that.

"I caught this from someone. Last week. It's scabies. I looked it up on the Internet."

"It's just a little blood test."

"It's not to me." OK, now my eyes were brimming with tears. That was definitely not good. The camera pulled back for a medium shot. I could see it all clearly: two understandably chagrined men regarded me pityingly, wondering why they'd ever gone in for this volunteer stuff to begin with, what with cranks like me wandering in from the cold. How could I explain to them that all blood tests had become inextricably entwined with AIDS tests for me? That I just couldn't stick out my arm and make a fist on a moment's notice? Every time I did it the silhouette of the hanging judge rose up behind the doctor's shoulder. I needed to make careful preparations for the occasion. I needed time to rummage through my survival kit for a bad-news strategy: stoic acceptance, or, of-course-I-didn't-have-it-so-what-was-I-worried-about; anything to keep the wolves out of the yard. I knew that I was being unreasonable. I knew, I knew, I knew. Nobody knew better than me.

I probably could have told them all that. They were, after all, gay men. But I'd never had to describe this particular dread because I'd never been subject to a pop blood test before. The fear just marauded through me, blind, inarticulate. Still, some filament of clarity burned with the message that if I was going to get out of there with my prescription for pesticide and without a bandage in the crook of my arm, I was going to have to pretend to be a reasonable person, something I was relatively expert at, something I'd had to do every day of my life from about the age of five. "Look," I said, faking an easy smile at the good doctor, since my syphilis was fait accompli for Igor. "Tell you what. You give me a prescription for the scabies medicine and I promise to come back next week and get a blood test if this hasn't cleared up."

"I really wish you'd have a blood test now."

"Look, you yourself just said that you can't catch tertiary syphilis." I was explaining this to them now in calm, slow-learner cadences. "I caught this from somebody. His symptoms are identical to mine. This could be scabies. Couldn't it?"

He looked up, searching the ceiling for the answer, smiled again, tolerantly said, "Yes." I watched him consider me. I watched him peer through the lace sheers of my docile little act and see the stubborn fright lurking behind them. I watched him realize there was no way a needle was coming within squirting distance of my arm that night. "OK. I'll write you a scrip. But if this hasn't cleared up by next week, you have to promise to come back and have the blood test."

"Deal." He didn't reach for the Mont Blanc and the pad corsaged into his lab-coat pocket. He seemed to be scanning me for signs that I wasn't the kind to welsh on a deal, especially a deal in which I was a potentially communicable menace. I tried to look like a person of quiet integrity until I couldn't stand it for one more second. "Deal, deal, deal. Cross my heart and hope not to die."

He reached. He wrote. He tore.

Candy Striper didn't take it like a sport. Vanity wounded, he turned on his heel and barreled out the door in search of other poor bastards to terrorize with more of his hysterical misdiagnoses.

Three days later, Wednesday night. My scabies were better, but far from gone. I veered, almost hourly, between the calm assurance that I was getting better and the absolute certainty that it was some bizarre AIDS-related syphilis, some mutant syphilis that was speeding on two wheels toward the charnel house. The trapdoors of it kept opening up under me and snatching my breath away. I checked my skin every ten or fifteen minutes, deciding that it looked better, it looked worse, that it didn't matter because we were all going to die anyway. Currents of panic swept me up and deposited me into lakes of despair, where I paddled around, contenting myself with fantasies of suicide. The real problem with suicide, as Dorothy Parker pointed out, was that there really wasn't an acceptable method.

Jump from a building?

Splat.

Ick.

A gun?

Same cosmetic complications.

A straight razor?

Ouch.

Pills?

No thanks. That usually meant drowning in your own vomit.

A car in a garage seemed reasonable, drifting gently away, like a balloon. But who had a car or a garage in New York? Oh sure, Trump and a few other capitalist overlords, but it wasn't exactly my crowd.

On some level I knew these weren't real fantasies because determined suicides overcame these objections all the time. For me, they were little alcoves tucked away inside my consciousness labeled IN CASE OF EMERGENCY, BREAK GLASS. They were what got me through the hours.

I called Jo Ann.

"Hi," she said, sounding happy to hear from me. Jo Ann usually sounded happy to hear from me, just as I was always happy to hear from her. Inexplicable love. How else would we limp through the battlefield, cradling our broken limbs?

"I think I'm dying."

"You're not dying." One day, I would be; but Jo Ann had agreed to hold my hand and so it was manageably terrifying.

"You wouldn't believe this itching."

"Yes, I would. I had it, remember?"

"I must have, like, sixty bites on my legs."

"You've got to stop this."

"How?"

"You've got to stop doing this to yourself."

"I know that, but I don't know how."

"You've just . . . got to. There isn't really any other choice."

Saturday night, about 7:00. I was sitting in the armchair of the living room with a very good bottle of red wine open in front of me. I'd decided, self-pityingly, to splurge. I'd had a rough week. If my young life was going to be cut short by scabies, then I was going to live it up. John was sunk in his usual segment of the couch. Ensure on the end table he wasn't even pretending to drink. Prescriptions everywhere. Cigarettes he had lit, and not touched, lay crushed in an ashtray. All the lights were off, except for the documentary flashing over us, a profile of Erik Estrada. It was a classic case of more-than-I-wanted-to-know. I think we were to the lean years, right before he got a Mexican soap opera. It was hard not to feel critical of and superior to and in general glad you weren't Erik Estrada, and I was imagining my own more dignified profile on Bravo or Ovation, the smart channels. A man with a bad haircut asking me questions in a probing British accent. Shots of me tousling the heads of my beloved dogs in my country kitchen as I sautéed something with sun-dried tomatoes in it. The likes of Susan Sontag and a subtitled Günter Grass speaking of my accomplishments with discreet but unmistakable admiration. A final pan of me thoughtfully chewing a pencil eraser at my solid mahogany desk, brow furrowed with *pensées*. Deep.

TV light is never flattering, but John looked particularly ghoulish, lost in a blanket except for the stump of his head. Still, they had let him out this afternoon, just as he'd promised; and now we were waiting for his sister to get in. Silently, unless you counted Erik and the mellow-toned narrator. I didn't. Pouring another glass of wine, I scratched my calf through my sweatpants, which provoked another storm of worry. I lit a cigarette to still it. Big help.

"So, your sister's coming, John."

He smiled at me.

"Are you excited?" I tried, desperate to distract myself from myself.

He nodded, still smiling, indulgently.

"How long's it been since you've seen her?"

"Oh, God, I don't know. A while."

"Are you guys close?"

He crossed his fingers. "Like this."

"Huh."

"We don't need . . . contact. It's one of the things I've learned from the Aquarians. When you're connected, you're connected."

"The who?"

"The Aquarians. Haven't you ever heard of us?" He sounded concerned.

Us. Him. Some zodiac thing. He was Aquarius. I had friends who would guess your sign. Nine times out of ten they were wrong. These people never believed in God, and yet they'd scrounge up the exact hour of their birth, along with a small fortune, to get some vegan chick who wore rings with Chinese symbols on them to do their charts. I never really understood it. They would say, "She told me I've always had trouble with men!" and I'd think, what, you didn't know that? Still, I knew better than to tangle with these types. One disparaging word and the next thing you knew they were calling you unevolved. I hated that because one way or another you knew they were right. It was like when people called you bourgeois back in the early seventies because you tied your shoes or drank a Coke every once in a while. It was the ultimate insult if you had aspirations to be anything other than a Kmart shopper. It was the "yo mama" of a certain set. Over time, of course, it turned out that we were all bourgeois, but you didn't know that then, so all you could do was issue public denials and vow silently to do better. I kind of miss those days now, when a large segment of the population actually thought it was bad to be materialistic and shallow and apolitical, before the days of fashion television. These days, to be shallow, materialistic, and apolitical is simply to be human.

"Oh," I said, "I'm a Libra." Libra was a coveted sign in the astrological world. We were supposed to be artistic, wonderful lovers, with a keen sense of justice. In my case, this just happened to be true.

"Not Aquarius. Aquarians." He looked at me scoldingly.

"Oh, yeah, Aquarians. I, do remember hearing something about that. It's like a. What?"

"It's a religion."

"Right." The game-show buzzer in my head was going off,

faintly, but that could have been for either the musical *Hair* or the 5th Dimension. *Up-Up and Away,* along with *The Cowsills,* had been my first two albums. I'd played them into rice paper. Some other gelatinous thought that wouldn't quite congeal was performing mitosis in my head. Anxiety began to nibble away at my cabernet calm. Cult. That was the word I was looking for. Brainwashing. Next thing you knew you were out at the airport wearing a curtain, peddling aphid-infested dandelions. OK. I hadn't bolted on John when plenty of other people would have. I hadn't had much choice. Still, I'd tried to be a good doobie. But that didn't include being strapped to a sacrificial stone slab with a ceremonial dagger poised above my heart. "You know, I was never really very clear about what the Aquarians believe in."

"It's more about what we don't believe in."

"Oh." That was novel. "Like what?"

"We don't believe in death. It doesn't exist."

"Well."

"We've got proof."

On TV, Erik Estrada's wife was talking about what a wonderful husband and father he was. How these days, he knew what was important — family. I sipped my wine. Wondering. I had to know. "What kind of proof?"

"Tapes. From the other side."

That wasn't computing. "Tapes?"

"Of Carol. She talks to us from the other side."

I can't say for certain that her name was actually Carol, but it was something equally dubious and banal. "Cassette tapes."

"Yeah."

"How do you record those, exactly?"

"They just do."

It always came down to that. Faith. As a child I'd been a fundamentalist Christian, much to my mother's discomfort. We'd only gone to church twice a year, once at Christmas, and once at Easter, after which we modeled our smart new outfits, our just-off-the-block haircuts, standing in front of the station wagon holding up Easter baskets for the Polaroid. But one Easter I got saved by the Right Reverend Farrell, a Chihuahua of a man who stoked his face prestroke red as he bombed us with his message: our imminent and endless damnation. I was eight. He was vivid. I was also a precocious physical coward who had no intention of writhing in a fire for two seconds, let alone eternity. I was his. This turned out to be a costly investment with long-term interest: once the Christians get their claws in you, you spend the rest of your life picking the fingernails from your shoulders. I basically spent the next several years with pamphlets held solemnly to my breast as I harassed shoppers at the mall up the road, asking if they had accepted Jesus Christ as their personal Lord and Savior. They took my pamphlets. What were they going to say to a pint-size proselytizer whose eyes were brimming with passionate concern? Buzz off, kid? Not in the South they weren't.

Later, when I discovered that homos — and I had always known, vaguely, that I was not like other little boys — were first in line for the cup of brimstone, I tried masturbating to girls, and prayed nightly, often tearfully, "to be ye made" whole. Masturbation, of course, was also a sin — that was a bit of conflict — but I figured desperate times, desperate measures. You wouldn't burn for beating off, as far as I could tell from Farrell's rants. After several years of that madness, I threw in my stained towel, and started doing things like dropping acid at Humble Pie concerts, which turned out to be an enormous consolation.

Once, during Bible class, I had the temerity to ask Farrell about the Indians. I knew for a fact from fourth-grade history that they hadn't heard the Word, because they had been riding their palominos around for quite a long time, in loincloths, spearing buffaloes, before we'd gotten here with It. I wanted to know what the contingency plan was. I was not being a smart mouth — I was devout. It had simply crossed my mind. If we'd been Catholic, there would have been a purgatory and a limbo. Problem solved. But we weren't. We were Southern Baptists, and Southern Baptists stuck to the basics. Heaven. Hell. Do not pass Go.

So. I asked a series of questions that began with the phrase, "But what about . . . ?" and Farrell stood there trying to answer until he finally bellowed, "Stand up!"

I did as I was told, keeping an eye on his hands, which he had been flexing into fists during our little exchange. As he often reminded us, he had killed a man with those very hands in a barroom brawl. If God could save the soul of a no-account, good-for-nothing, ex-con sinner like him, what made us so uppity as to think God couldn't save the likes of us? He'd toted that story out enough Sundays that you knew it was his favorite. It was not mine. I found it scary. It also made me sad. All I could think about was not the miracle of how God had saved a wretch like Farrell but rather the poor man he'd murdered. Here Farrell got to go off and be a preacher man in a wash-and-wear blue suit, whereas all his victim got was the life beat out of him until he was splayed across the pool table, ruining the green felt with his blood. If he hadn't been saved then he was Satan's bacon. It bothered me, but not enough to bring it up. I vaguely worked it out that he'd made it to heaven on some technicality that had something to do with being killed by a preacher.

There were quite a lot of stories like that in our church. These people had usually been excellent sinners of great stamina.

So I stood, hoping I wasn't going to be churned out as the next Sunday morning parable illustrating Farrell's temper and God's sweet forgiveness of it.

"Now," Farrell ordered. "Sit down."

Not wanting to take any chances, I did.

"What did you just do there?" he asked.

Panicky, I tried to figure out what I had just done. It was like digging around for that hall pass you know was in your pocket just three seconds ago and coming up with lint.

"What did you do?"

I was about a dozen hot gulping breaths from tears. "I don't know."

"You sat up, and you sat back down."

OK. I could have gotten that. Maybe that was my problem.

Maybe I was making things way more complicated than they had to be. My mother sometimes accused me of that. Grateful, I said, "Yeah."

"And when you sat back down, did you ask yourself if that chair was gonna hold you up?"

"No, sir."

"THAT'S FAITH, SON," he said, leaning in and pointing at me with his whole body.

So I knew about faith, son. It was the rock that the pick of reason couldn't break. If John thought he had tapes from the other side, then John had tapes from the other side. How did they make them? They just did.

"Oh," I said, not a skeptical "oh," more like, how very, very interesting.

Which only encouraged him. "We don't believe in AIDS either."

"Huh," I said, still monitoring tone for interest level and any stray chords of stark disbelief. They didn't believe in AIDS. That was interesting. I knew several extremely, you might even say radically, dead people who would be surprised, perhaps even pissed, to hear that AIDS had been something they could have had the luxury of not believing in. It was somehow insulting, as if all those dead people had brought it upon themselves because they hadn't had the fortitude to pooh-pooh away the blindness and the purple lakes slapped across their skin, the shriveling down to dust. Part of me knew that people who might be dying needed to believe what they needed to believe, whatever that was, to get them through the blank terror of it. But part of me wanted to leap from my chair, wrestle him to the floor, and twist his arm behind his back until he called uncle and admitted that AIDS was a fact, not a state of mind.

"I have a picture of Jesus that bleeds healing oils," he said. "Would you like to see it?"

OK. Where was the hidden camera? Where was Alan Funt? Boy, they had really gone through a lot of trouble for one lousy stunt. I mean getting Cabrini in on it was the limit. Come on. The only people who had pictures of Jesus that bled healing oils were tiny Italian widows in black kerchiefs who lived in remote mountain villages. Or sun-shrunken geezers in Kentucky who'd had one snakebite too many back out at the revival tent.

John was smiling at me, but it wasn't the you're-on-*Candid-Camera* variety. It was the hopeful smile of somebody who smelled a convert.

"Uh, OK."

He jack-in-the-boxed from the couch, and I poured another glass of wine. His bedroom door squeaked open. I glanced over to see what Erik Estrada was up to. Nothing good. I lit another cigarette, hoping this would be the one that would restore my cracked equilibrium. No such luck.

John dialed up the dimmer switch and suddenly light was everywhere you looked. I don't mean that in a good way. It wasn't a living room that could withstand that kind of scrutiny. Frayed cushions. A chair leg patched with duct tape. Scratches on nearly every surface. John stepped around the side of my chair, the painting in front of him like some lunatic's placard about the end being near.

It was. A Jesus-on-velvet head shot. I sipped my wine several times. Then I switched to smoking thoughtfully for a little variation. I think I'd somehow been expecting something more Byzantine, something tiled and ancient. Not this. Don't get me wrong. It was a good Jesus-on-velvet painting, if there is such a thing. I mean, it looked like all the other ones I'd ever seen, and where I come from, I'd seen plenty. But it seemed, even after I factored in my genetic inclination for hysterical overreaction, tragic. I'm sorry. There are no possible metaphors here. There are no metaphors because it was already a metaphor for everything that was cheap and degraded and yet also embodied the deepest longing for transcendence from the muck and the sorrow and the crumminess of life. I didn't find it the least bit funny, and I was ashamed to be reminded, with chest-thumping force, of what a condescending fuck I was.

"It's great," I said, taking another nervous sip. Given my background, I found it hard to lie with You-Know-Who staring me down. Friends who know my taste have often given me things like baby Jesus night-lights. Camp. I get rid of them as soon as that friend is out the door, before the divine lightning has a chance to reach down and smite me. No kidding.

"It is great," John said, his voice awash with the passionate attachment of the true believer.

"How does it, how does it make the oil?"

"I don't know. It just does. I collect it sometimes at night in these little vials."

"So, you've actually seen it, make the oils?"

"Oh yeah." Emphatic nodding.

I guess most people would have thought, nut job. But some fragrance had perfumed the apartment on certain nights when I'd come home from work, something too pungently thick and sweet and . . . oily. I'd assumed it was some wretched cologne Alan had doused himself with to set the boys sniffing. So I was willing to consider it for a moment. Besides, life might just be strange enough to accommodate oils trickling from a velvet painting.

I have had, consistently, or consistently enough, interludes that take on the quality of the miraculous. They're usually pretty simple. I'll be sitting, say, at a bar; and the moment will begin to dawn, all the foldings and unfoldings, the origami of history, the personal and the impersonal, my grandfather the farmer, the Revolutionary War, that led me to be here with all these other people who had been led here too by the myriad happenstance of their own lives, all the sedimented accumulations — the smoke and the cologne and the grease, all the amber of the past layered in fly wings and sand dollars and spent Bic pens, the man who discovered how to make red light emanate from the jukebox blasting Elvis Costello, along with Jonas Salk and his polio vaccine — someone would not have been here without it, perhaps even me — not to mention that lime grown in California, now a mangled wedge in someone's half-finished gin and tonic, all of it, all of us, stitched together in this little knot of time, and even the fact of the dawning itself, there, inside of me, how many angels were dancing on the head of the pin of this moment, how could such radical complexity be an accident? It couldn't. It was only that the designs within the designs within the designs sometimes looked like chaos. Healing oils from a velvet Jesus? Sure. Why not?

"So, are you using them?" I said.

He nodded again, a little too vehemently, and I knew why: they weren't working; he knew it.

"I wish I could rub some on my career," I said.

"You'd be surprised," he said, dead serious, hauling the painting back to his room.

We sat silently after that, watching some Whoopi Goldberg movie from the mideighties that would have been a crime in a properly run culture. Nothing against Whoopi Goldberg. It had not been a good period for her. John coughed intermittently. It was nothing more than your average smoker's hack, but every time he did it, my heart did a disco step. It made it hard to smoke with any real pleasure. Also, the wine was not working. Instead of the connoisseur's calm I'd hoped for, I was listing toward melancholy.

How could that Whoopi Goldberg movie bear to be in the same room with the mystery and cruelty of John's dying? It seemed like we should have been chanting something low and primitive to appease our own dread, that we should have been robed and hooded, in a fog of incense, possibly slitting the throats of lambs, crying wretchedly out to God as we tore at our hair. We should not be watching this movie. Bring back the velvet Jesus, I wanted to cry out. Make it bleed. Let us rub the all-too-temporary temples of our bodies with its oils. But that moment had already passed, and in my heart I knew I could not bring myself to be in thrall to a painting that looked like it had been bought in the art department at Wal-Mart.

I once knew a young man who'd said, "I'm too scared to die. I don't know how to do it." As it turned out, he hadn't had to do anything. A few days later, it had simply dragged him, speechless, into its lair. But that was the problem. We, none of us, knew how to do it. It was all improvisation. I didn't know how to die either, but I knew we should not be watching this movie. I could feel it trivializing us into another kind of nonexistence, where all our souls came in café colors and were plastered in decals.

Fortunately, the doorman buzzed. John's sister. Maybe she could save us.

I'm going to call her Becky because I once knew a Becky, and John's sister could have been that Becky's stunt double. John did another of his startling antelope-leaps from the couch and ripped the door from its hinges. It was one of those flashes when I thought, this man does not have cancer complicated by HIV. Becky dropped her aquamarine, floral-printed luggage on the floor and they crushed themselves into each other, squealing. I stood up, the way I'd been raised to, and waited to shake her hand, a real smile pinned to my face. My blues were sifting away in the bright colander of their filial love, nothing like the restrained back patting my family doled out.

Becky was a big gal. Some people, like Mr. McNally, to use an unfair example, look fat. Lumbering, breathless in their baggy clothes, they end up drawing attention to the very thing they're most self-conscious of. But other people, people like Becky, inhabit their bodies in such a way that they seem naturally large. They wear brightly patterned clothes that fit; they swoop around effortlessly. There's something impeccable about them. You never think of them as fat.

I used to work with a girl, Marie, who was also a big gal. Marie had big tits, big hips, and big lips that she painted cannibal red. Her hair, though it had to be dyed, was some radiant blond. There was something Germanic about her, and I mean horned-hat-about-to-hurl-a-spear Germanic; but she was so funny and kind that she wasn't the least bit frightening. She used to zoom past me at the club where we both worked — she was the busiest and most efficient person I've ever met — and say, "Wesley, do not think about 'Muskrat Love,'" effectively trapping that song in my head, where it would whirl for the rest of the shift. On the one hand, you wanted to strangle her. On the other, it seemed like the cleverest trick ever. With the possible exception of Tina Turner — and folks, if you ever see her live, bring the buckets you'll have to be carried out in after your meltdown — Marie was the sexiest person, man or woman, I've ever seen in the flesh, with all of the flesh's dreamy possibilities. Straight men practically fainted in her presence, what with the blood rushing from their heads into their instant erections.

OK, Becky was no Marie; but she was stylish in a way I could never hope to be. She was an accessorizing mama, doing things with broaches and scarves and fringe that would have left me looking like a window treatment after the big quake. She had that thing large women dread being told they have: a pretty face. But she did have a pretty face, with a smile that looked like it could have powered a small city. Her hair was dyed a sunny blond. She had the conquering air of a superhero.

After she was finished with John, she charged over to me, hand extended, and said, "Wesley or Alan?"

Finally. Finally. The cavalry had arrived.

I got a job teaching at the Gotham Writer's Workshop. My first class was Saturday, noon, which I later learned was the absolute bottom of the barrel. All the new kids had it shoved down their throats.

I actually liked teaching. I had plenty of artist friends who didn't. Go be a greeter down at the Wal-Mart, I'd think when I heard them bitching about the hours, the students, the money. For someone like me, who'd been programmed for minimum wage, forty skull-clubbing hours a week, it seemed miraculous that you could squeak by on twenty hours just talking about writing. Which I really did find interesting, even when it was bad. Trying to figure out how to make a story work was a puzzle I enjoyed putting together. I liked the transaction of it, the osmosis of what I knew becoming what they knew.

Most people want to write because they're sad. That really is true. Our feelings often stalk us, ruthless and determined as contract killers, and if we could somehow etch our particular sadness into glass, the light might shine through the spidery lines of it in LSD trails of prismatic beauty. We want a record. We don't want to pass unnoticed into the silent mob of the dead. We don't want to become our photographs — that, and nothing more. I felt I understood that, even when my students didn't know their semicolons from their rectal colons.

Of course there were the people who just wanted to write a potboiler so they could ride the rest of life out on a magic carpet of cash. Their feelings were deep too, in a seven-deadly-sins sort of way: greed, envy, a localized desire to be the subject of a *People* magazine spread. They always seemed to be filled with lunatic optimism and a balls-to-the-wall determination that would have been chilling in a normal person. But they wanted to be writers, and in my experience, writers — let's just go whole hog and say most artists — were not particularly normal people. They were this bunch of freaks standing in the middle of the busy intersection, frantically waving their arms and yelling, "STOP. EVERYONE. I HAVE SOMETHING VITALLY, VITALLY IMPORTANT TO TELL YOU." It made some of them crazy, some of them bitter, and many of them into the kind of cutthroat careerists who would have made Eve, as in *All About,* look like somebody who wasn't really giving it her best shot. By comparison, even my most ambitious students still had a certain beginner's charm.

I had gotten this job by begging an art-colony acquaintance I'd run into at an opening. He taught there. I'd learned long ago that naked desperation, a fairly steady companion of mine, worked better than when I tried to be a suave operator who could smooth talk his way around the chutes and ladders of success. *That* Wesley ended up sounding like Eddie Haskell — That's a lovely dress you're wearing, Mrs. Cleaver — and people understandably recoiled from him. I recoiled from him.

The interview was about eight hours long and was conducted by one of the two young men who owned Gotham. They were both about ten years my junior. Everyone at Gotham, it seemed, was ten years my junior. I was getting to the age when people who actually were younger looked younger still. Twenty-year-olds looked ten to me; and they all seemed to have a terrible-twos sort of energy, hurtling around with a pointless enthusiasm that was pure novocaine to a bum like me. I'd stand there in the office, numbly trying to figure out how to Xerox a Lorrie Moore story I wanted to go over, while they swarmed around me, e-mailing, faxing, cell phoning, instant messaging, saving, deleting, cut and pasting, beaming via satellite for all I knew. I could tell they thought I was weird in a gay-old-geezer sort of way. They didn't think my vintage overcoats looked retro and spiffy, but like something from the Boone's Farm Wino Collection. I hated to acknowledge how close to the mark that was. I was about two unsteady steps from the sheer drop of homelessness. As John went, so went my fortunes.

Gotham rented classrooms in various buildings, like AA. My first was in an elementary school in the West Village. In the lobby, Gotham workers sat at folding tables, handing out packets and MasterCarding people. An eastern European–

looking man in a green janitor's uniform sat behind a reception desk, reading a paper with words that looked more like a wallpaper design than news of the world. Beside him, on the floor, a little boy, who I assumed was his son, was playing toy trucks, crashing them into each other, rolling them up the side of his father's chair. I was handed my own fat teaching packet, which turned out to contain lots of exclamatory advice that I knew I wouldn't be capable of following on how to conduct the class. Exclamation points made me nervous. Punctuation-wise, I was more of an ellipsis-type person.

My classroom smelled like art paste and Fantastik. Maybe third grade? There was a fish tank, and beside the fish tank was a large piece of paper on which the students had crayoned rules concerning the fish. DO NOT TAP THE GLASS, DO NOT PICK UP THE FISH, DO NOT EAT THE FISH, and other sorts of sensible advice. The bulletin board had autumn things cut out of construction paper stapled to it: pumpkins, a haystack. The teacher had a bouquet of dried corn on the edge of her desk. I wondered if children who lived in the West Village had ever even seen a haystack, and that got me to wondering about how fall might really translate into construction paper for them; but the only things I could think of were so sordid that I was saddened by how corrupt I'd become.

I had four students — three black women and a very large white man I'm going to call Fred. Two of the black women, Tryphine and Ngong, were African. The other black woman was named Mai and had just moved back from Florida. Tryphine and Ngong were both very dark, but Tryphine was plump and wore kerchiefy, African-looking things, whereas Ngong was angular, wore wire rims, and dressed like a nice Connecticut lady who might bring us all egg-salad sandwiches some afternoon. Mai was not angular but twig-thin. She was light skinned and also wore glasses, plastic designer ones that made a statement. Glasses with exclamation points. She dressed like a frat boy: khaki pants, a white button-up shirt with the sleeves rolled up. I was almost certain she was a lesbian, but she began nattering away, almost immediately, about some boyfriend, like she'd guessed that I'd tried to peg her.

Mai was, to put it mildly, a chatterbox. Watching her talk was like watching someone drive an obstacle course in one of those expensive-car commercials. She'd veer here, there, never hit the brakes. In about ten minutes we'd all learned that she rented a house in Jersey, was a recovering alcoholic, worked for a start-up dot-com, had a boyfriend about twenty years her junior, was about forty-five herself, had been a drug dealer's girlfriend back in Florida, was sort of psychic, and baskets of other info that would have taken a lifetime to learn about a normal person. Mai was fascinating and exhausting. I wondered what kind of chemical imbalance coursed through a person who had to take every corner on two wheels? As a student, she was already a problem, since there didn't seem to be any way to shut her up, short of surgically wiring her jaw shut. I smiled pleasantly, raised my eyebrows, and chuckled at the proper moments. Fred also feigned an interest. Ngong studied Mai like she was a rare specimen, a giant bug who had mastered sign language. Tryphine paid her no mind, just thumbed through the pages of her own manuscript, scribbling notes to herself in the margins. Finally I threw myself in front of Mai, slamming her to a halt. I half-expected to see an air bag blossom from the table in front of her.

The first class was good. We went over a disturbing-in-a-good-way story by Fred concerning a man who ends up falling from the top of an Aztec temple in Mexico, a modern-day sacrifice of sorts. Tryphine and Ngong liked it too. Naturally it reminded Mai of her vacation in Acapulco a few years back when she and her then boyfriend, the rock star, not the drug dealer, had been forced to stand naked in the ocean, at gunpoint, while thieves had bundled their things up into the beach towels with giant margaritas printed on them — this was when she still drank — that they had just bought in town. We never found out if Mai liked the story or not, but we all agreed that the Acapulco experience sounded harrowing.

That Tuesday I got home from Telesessions to find John and his sister in a sinister wonderland. Some Christmas album was playing. I don't remember which one, but it was something heart freezing, like *A Very Brady Christmas*. I opened that door and reared back, like the room was a deranged motorcycle gang, headed straight for me.

I have a pronounced sense of unreality. Normal things, something as simple as a woman in a khaki skirt inspecting a frog-shaped bank in front of a grocery cart stacked with plaid

flannel shirts, can whiplash through me. It can make me so
nervous that I begin to get this trembly feeling, like the edges
of my skin are vibrating, like my heart is a dolphin. The
armpits of my shirt go sticky as honey. I feel like, OK, wait a
minute, here we all are on this rock whirling and orbiting in
the middle of outer space, and where did orbiting even come
from, this great star of disintegrating heat that we're just far
enough away from so that instead it makes lilies and algae
and the person suddenly gripped with this terror, not to mention some psycho who slits open women's bellies so he can
fuck them in the appendix, which is just for starters, what
about some regular guy who traded his records in for CDs
when that came along, and whose favorite show was *Cheers*
until that was canceled, but then there was *Seinfeld,* OK, so
he buys his aftershave and has this girlfriend who's the host-
ess at T.G.I. Friday's, and then finally dies of testicular cancer
when he's thirty-nine, what about that shit, and I think, how
can you just be standing there picking up that frigging frog
bank in your khaki skirt, what is wrong with us, I mean I'm
just standing here behind you, a box of unfrozen Freezie Pops
under my arm because they were on sale for, OK, it was an
incredible price, a buck ninety-nine for a box of one hundred,
but what the fuck?

Have you ever wanted to scream like that?

Probably not. Still, I think just about anybody would have
been shaken by the sight of his apartment, in October,
draped, blanketed, drenched in lights, an orgy of them, twinkling lavender and yellow and green, garlands of plastic
mistletoe slung across walls, looped through the backs of the

dining-room chairs, crawling across the back of the couch, angels and Santa Clauses and mangers and characters from *Peanuts,* battalions of them, either blinking or glowing from within, or splattered with gemstones of light from without. A little fake tree on the coffee table, about the size of a toddler. It was pornographic. If the Grinch had shown up, I would have pinned the Legion of Honor to his furry breast.

John sat, smiling, gums red as wassail, in a green elf's hat trimmed in fur. It bent in the way those hats do, and the little matching ball dangled by his chin. Very traditional. He was wearing a spanking-new, extralong *Cathy*-cartoon T-shirt for a nightgown, which he'd tucked his legs inside. You could see his gaunt feet. Those were pure Halloween.

Becky was smiling hysterically. She was in full Becky drag, a shawl pinned around her by a poinsettia broach the size of my fist. She'd turned up the volume of her hair and makeup to holiday decibels. She didn't look bad, just harrowingly perfect, like she'd popped in from the Sears catalog, and might best be viewed from about fifty paces.

All around them was the carnage of opened presents.

"Merry Christmas," Becky said, jolly as a shopping-mall Santa.

"Uh, hi." Sorry. Couldn't do it. Christmas was that time of year when the world conspiracy to bring me to grief operated at peak efficiency. I must have looked like I'd stumbled onto the site of a mass grave.

"We decided to celebrate a little early this year," she said, a little more tentatively.

"Oh."

They both continued smiling at me. I tried to smile back, but the muscles in my face were refusing to cooperate.

"Look what John got me." She held up the crystal figurine of an angel you could have bludgeoned the pope with.

"Wow. That's. Very nice." Completely unconvincing, which made me feel rotten, because who was I to make people feel bad about their Christmas in October? My mother always used to say that I thought I was better than everybody, and I guess she was really onto something there. I only wished that it made me happier.

"And I got this," John said, striking a model's pose in his *Cathy* nightshirt. "I picked it out." Then he coughed, explosively. It whacked him forward and bent him over. Becky patted his back, looking over at me and shaking her head, not smiling for the first time since I'd met her. I shrugged, shook my own head. What was the correct gesture for a moment like this? Who even knew there were going to be moments like this? When he was finally through, his eyes were teary from the strain of it.

"Better, sweetie?" she said.

He nodded, tried to squirm back into a comfortable position. The life had gone out of both of them.

"Well," I said, "guess I should hit the old sack" — something I never said, but somehow hoping a folksy tone would rescue us all from this moment.

"You know what?" Becky said, slapping her thighs, "I haven't seen your room yet."

"Oh. OK. It's really not much to look at."

"Oh, I bet it's just wonderful."

"Yeah, well. It's home." Except, of course, it wasn't.

She followed me back.

I lit the place up, threw my backpack on the bed, had a look around myself. Dear God. Who was this person? What did he have other than a few books, a boom box on the radiator, and a doddering computer? Becky, a Martha Stewart centerfold who'd pulled the staple from her belly and sprung to life, was probably thinking, poor kid. But she said, loudly, "This is great, great. So many books. Have you read all these?"

The truth was, I hadn't, maybe even only a quarter of them. I bought books all the time, thinking one day I'd get around to them, and I usually did in my stumbling fashion. I'd recently read *The Haunting of Hill House* by Shirley Jackson, a little paperback I'd picked up for a quarter from a thrift store, like, six years ago. But I was suddenly ashamed to be a person who had very little but books, and didn't even read those, so I said, "Yes." Maybe she'd think I was poor and noble and destined for greatness after my death.

"I'm a big reader," she said, but I knew she wasn't. People who were big readers never said that.

She took me by the wrist — her skin was soft as a fresh doughnut — and whispered, "I think John thinks he won't be here for Christmas." Tears were already helplessly forming in her eyes.

"And what do you think?" I said, low.

She shrugged, but it was the kind of shrug you use when

you can't bring yourself to say yes, you thought so too. That's when it hit me: he was going to die, wasn't he? It was an idea I'd been circling almost from the first day I'd moved in, but that's all I'd done — circle it. I'd been throwing him these little life preservers in my mind: when he went to the hospital that first time; when Alan finally confronted him; now that Becky was here. But no. All the life preservers were the cheap, kiddie kind that went flat after a few hours in the pool. He was going to die, really and truly and deeply; and I was going to be homeless; and the thousands of dollars I'd thrown at this place were going to be lowered into the ground with him. Comparatively I was the lucky one here, but only by comparison.

"Why won't he do the chemotherapy?"

She shook her head, she didn't know, beyond speech. The tears were coming at a clip now, gliding effortlessly over her flawlessly prepared face. Her mascara did not run; it must have been top-dollar stuff. Her head fell slowly, *tiiimberrr,* to my shoulder, and then shook there. I rubbed her back through her slick shawl. She wore nice perfume, something vanilla with floral accents, discreet but solidly there, like the middle-class conviction that everyone else was godless. Her hair, frozen with mousse, sanded at my chin. It was an awful moment, because you knew that this was a woman who had mown down the crises of her life, a bulldozer of optimism; but she wouldn't be able to micromanage or delegate this away. My heart broke for her, but I was also thinking, I'm fucked, no lube, no condom, just flat-out fucked. Here a man was dying and his sister was sobbing on my shoulder and all I could think about were my own sad prospects. I'd joined the Gambino family of my New York friends. I was a made man.

On Wednesday, when I got home from work, Becky was already asleep on the foldout couch. I crept past her into the kitchen for my usual post-Telesessions nightcap. From Alan's room, the underwater murmur of people fucking but trying to keep it quiet. This was no time for manners. I rapped on the slats of his folding door. He went, "Hmmmm?" his voice still stuck in the honey of his fucking.

"Alan," I whispered, harshly, "it's Wesley. We need to talk."

"Hmmmm?"

"We need to talk. Now."

A disgruntled "Uhhhmmm."

The groan of somebody pulling out and not being very happy about it. Some moaning talking smooching. Then the door rattled open and Alan was standing there in a towel and his mangled hair. His body was everything it had promised to be, and I felt like breaking the vodka bottle over my head for being aroused by the sight of him at that wretched moment. What kind of a low-life pervert was I?

There was no point in messing around. "John's dying."

"I, uh, know. I talked to his, sister." He was still struggling to the surface.

"What are we going to do?"

"What do you mean?"

"About the apartment."

That slapped him awake. "Man, I don't know. I really don't know. I, I, I can't fucking think about this."

"Look. A couple of my friends, mercenary types, real killers, said maybe we could get the apartment ourselves." In the mirror, I was still recognizably human; but the icy and amphibious blood of a New Yorker trying to survive was beginning to course through my veins.

"OK. OK. Uh. I met this lawyer a few weeks ago. I think I still got his card around here somewhere. Maybe I could call him."

"Do it."

"OK. I'll . . . do it tomorrow."

I slithered past Becky in the dark. A box of moonlight made a picture of her from the shoulders up. Her nightgown, pink and lacy, was scalloped across the freckled milk of her bosom like wedding-cake frosting. Her mouth was half-open in a frown and her brow was furrowed. In sleep, all the bluster was gone. She looked sad and bewildered.

Calling Jo Ann had become a nightly event, and I saw no reason to stop now.

"Hello?" Jo Ann said sharply.

"Are you all right?"

"Oh, it's just Sheba." Sheba was Jo Ann's sixteen-year-old collie. They had this endless conversation going in which Jo Ann said Sheba's name a lot in various tones while Sheba responded with sorrowful stares, hopeful wags of her tail, and the occasional excited yip. It was more than the usual pet/owner thing. It was more like two sisters who'd been rattling around the same house in bed slippers for a very long time.

"Me and Alan are looking into getting the apartment."

"Weird."

"You mean creepy."

"No, I mean weird. Creepy is when you're sprinkling rat poison in their scrambled eggs so you can get the apartment. You're not doing that, are you?"

"I'm not that far gone yet. Besides, wouldn't rat poison turn up in the autopsy?"

"It always does in the true-crime books, but then I guess people who get away with it aren't exactly crowing about it in some bestseller."

"You just wait."

As it turned out, I didn't have to worry about the ethics of getting John to put me on the lease. On Thursday, as I was leaving for work, he barreled into the apartment, Becky on his heels. He was choking. She looked utterly grim and was shaking her head. They flew past me into his bedroom, where I could hear him retching. I felt like I'd just watched a train derail.

Alan had talked to his lawyer/trick. Yes, it was possible that we could get our names on the lease; but then we might also be liable for certain debts. No fucking way, Alan had said. He'd just gotten out from under all that shit. When I asked him what he was going to do, he sighed miserably and said, "I don't know."

Neither did I, but I did call the Gay Roommating Service. As it turned out, my hundred or so bucks had bought me the right to their list for six months. I waited to feel some small measure of relief. It never showed up.

By Friday afternoon I had an appointment to look at the apartment of some guy I'm going to call Joe because I remember thinking at the time that it sounded like the nice, normal name of someone who wouldn't die after a few months while their picture of Jesus bled oils at you. Then again, there was John's name, and where had that gotten me?

Joe's room in his apartment wasn't exactly a deal. Seven-fifty a month. But you didn't have to pay utilities, so there was that. The price was about what every other room was going for. I was attracted to it because it was downtown, around Seventeenth and Third, where most of my life took place. My favorite bar was easily within late-night impulse range. It felt like a neighborhood. It didn't have the frenzied, moneyed feel of the Upper East Side; and it also didn't look like you'd have your throat slit if you had to run to the deli for a pack of smokes at 3:00 in the morning. I allowed myself a twinge of hope.

The building had been built in the sixties and had these odd glass columns in the foyer, lit from within, with plastic gemstones the size of brains stuck to them. Sort of czarist/Fred Flintstone. I knew they'd make me happy every time I saw them. The halls and elevator were spotlessly clean and flawlessly quiet. Maybe after I'd been there for a year I could find my own place on another floor. A joint this big had to have turnover. When Joe opened the door I was imagining a woman playing the harp in the corner of my studio apartment near a vase of fresh orchids while Fran Leibowitz and I traded quips.

He was a pear-shaped guy, about my age, with wavy, shoulder-length black hair, wisped gray. You could still make out the faded letters of a technological company on his T-shirt.

"Oh," he said, tugging at his jeans, "hi."

"Hi," I said in my best supersalesman's voice, shoving out my hand. He shook it, kind of.

"Come in," he said sadly, like he was inviting in a terminal illness.

Down the centimeter of a foyer. To the left, a kitchenette so new it looked like it had just come from the loading dock. The living room was a couch, a coffee table, a TV, and a double bed with a Japanese screen in front of it. There was no floor to speak of. Or there were these trickles of floor. A person from a two-dimensional world would have been perfectly happy living there. I will never know how Joe, who was far from flat, managed it. He sat, with a sigh, on the edge of the bed.

Oh, yeah. I forgot. On every available surface were G.I. Joe–like dolls in every conceivable form of dress, like his own private "It's a Small World after All." Except in this small world everyone had a giant, erect cock sculpted to the sexless place that is usually a doll's naughty bits. I'm guessing there were about three hundred of them, but it would have been like guessing jelly beans in a glass jar.

"So, tell me about yourself," he said with a complete lack of interest.

Trying to ignore the three hundred or so doll dicks pointing at me, I went into my spiel. Quiet as a church mouse. Neat as a pin. Like a Muhammad Ali poem. He didn't care if I smoked. We'd covered that on the phone. I loved to cook. Didn't mind sharing. I had this wonderful new teaching job that paid a fortune. Given the cramped quarters, I threw in that I was never there, a bonus prize, like something you'd get with the cereal. To hear me tell it I was so busy I had to check my planner to see when it was time to take the next breath. He could sue me later when he found out I never left my room.

"OK," he said, at 78 rpm.

Then, nothing, long enough for me to get nervous and say, nodding my head toward the nearest prick, "These are interesting."

The mention of his obsession did not brighten him up. "I special-order them from a woman who makes them in San Francisco. They're about three hundred dollars a piece."

Some quick math told me that that came to about a hundred grand. "They're neat," I lied.

"This is my room. I guess you want to see yours."

"That would be great."

He stood up with all the energy and cheer of an anvil. OK. So he slept in the living room. So he made most installation artists look like rank amateurs. So the apartment was the size of a coffin. So he wasn't exactly a comedy club. It was at least one evolutionary step up from a cardboard box in Central Park. It wasn't John's and that made it seem like the Dakota.

That is, until we squeezed ourselves into my room. There was a single mattress on the floor, dresser for a headboard. At least a hundred black-and-white photos, expensively framed and lit like Hurrell — museum-quality printing — covered the walls like ivy from a fairy tale. I guess you'd call them high-end porn, things like some naked guy, armored in muscles, gazing sensitively off stage left as he sat on a large rock in the middle of a river.

"I'd need to keep the chest of drawers in here," he said.

"Well, I do have a couple of things I'd like to move in. And these pictures. Uh, what about them?"

"What do you mean? It's my collection."

"So I'd get to keep them up?" I said, trying for the best possible spin.

He nodded. I had another look around. Given my insomnia, a tiny bunny in the middle of a nighttime forest surrounded by hundreds of lamp-lit and predatory feline eyes would have a better chance of sleep. "Have you ever thought about storage?"

"No," he said, like what kind of a philistine was I?

"I was just thinking they might keep better."

He scratched his head. "Uh, look, this probably isn't going to work out."

"Why not?" I said, my voice glittering with panic and forced gaiety. OK, I didn't want to live in this smut shop either, but if I couldn't convince this weirdo that I was a desirable roommate, I had this sudden elevator-drop feeling in my stomach that I'd be sleeping with the pigeons.

"I don't know. It's just a feeling I have."

"Talk to me here. Maybe you've gotten the wrong impression about me."

He shook his head no with a grim little smile and gestured, palm up, toward the bedroom door, the universal sign for this is the way out, bub.

"You know," I said, "I think you should keep me in mind, just in case. I mean that's just common sense."

"There are already a couple of guys ahead of you. Really cute guys."

"You know, I think I could be very attractive if I lost ten pounds, did something with my hair, got a tattoo." Nothing. Just the caveman back of his neck leading me down the hall. "That was a joke."

"Hmmm . . . That was the bathroom," he said as we passed it.

"Maybe I should have a look at that."

"Nah. What for?"

He opened the front door and stood there, sentry.

"So what is it?" I asked.

"What?"

"Why don't you want me to move in here?"

"It's nothing personal."

"When somebody says that, it's always personal. It's like the old relationship conversation, it's-not-you-it's-me. Except it is them."

"Hey, look, we're never going to see each other again."

"But if you tell me what it is, it might help me with the next place."

"I don't know what it is. It's just a feeling."

"What kind of a feeling?"

"You're not . . . I don't know, gay enough."

"Huh?"

"I mean, you're gay, but the guy who rents the room now, he gets fistfucked. It's like, I understand that."

"Huh."

"You know what I mean?"

"No."

"Look, I'm a normal gay guy and it's really important that I be around somebody who's . . . gay. You seem, you just seem like you'd be happier living with somebody else."

"Like who?"

"Somebody different. I'm HIV and, I don't know, I think your energy would really bring me down. I have to be really careful about that. I've already been sick once."

"Oh." This conversation was just getting worse and worse. Now I wasn't just an undesirable tenant but a potential threat to his immune system. And yet I thought I understood, in some vague cove of my mind, what he meant about me. I was . . . different. I wasn't queer in the right way. I wasn't queer as in dance beats and back rooms and workouts. Alan was, and that's exactly why John hadn't liked him. That's why he had liked me. John and I were both . . . what? Odd, I guess.

Joe stood there, just inside his apartment, and there I was, not a foot away, but the doorframe between us may as well have been the sheer face of a cliff because I was in the hall. He was the man with three hundred dicks and he'd somehow convinced himself that he was normal, whatever that means. In some rarefied way, I suppose he was.

"I will keep you in mind," he said. "You never know."

"Right," I said, never failing to be touched when someone lied to spare your feelings.

Joe was right about me, of course. I couldn't get anything right, not even being gay, which you might have thought would have been a genetic cinch.

I once had a job interview to teach in the University of Alabama's graduate creative writing program. For those of you who've never taught college, there's this group called the Modern Language Association, the professional organization of mostly English professors. Once a year they have a big meeting where they present papers on topics so obscure that to the average intelligent person they would sound like the mumblings of a lunatic. At the two I attended there also seemed to be lots of extracurricular adultery. At first that seemed sad in the way closet drinkers are sad. Then I really thought about the idea of two scholars, released from the Chaucer mines where they pickaxed the tenses of Middle English verbs, now drunk on the minibar and going at it on the hotel sheets. It seemed sort of sweet.

Anyway, they also interview candidates for department jobs at these things and this one was in New York. I was staying with friends in Soho and the day before the big interrogation, I'd nabbed an African scarf from a parking-lot flea market. I don't know how African the scarf actually was, but it was thickly blue and I liked the heavy texture from the feels I could cop through its plastic wrapper. The next day I thought, what the hell, and threw it on as a kind of declaration that I had a personality under all this M.L.A. gear. As I walked to the midtown hotel where the interviews were being held, I kept scouting for glimpses of myself in the gigantic plate-glass windows of the stores and banks. It was a bleak day, drizzly and cold, the kind of sky that bruised everything it brushed blue-gray, like a corpse in a movie. Still, I thought I looked pretty spiffy.

In the lobby, a mull of the other candidates, reading something like *Verb Journal*. Most of them visibly uncomfortable. There was a lot of nervous throat clearing and discreet sniffs at their armpits. Their accessories were making me nervous. Too many grown women in barrettes. The men favored these half-shoe/half-boot things that zipped and were disconcertingly elfish. I made for the elevator before I caught whatever fashion virus was going around out there.

In the room, three people were arranged in a semicircle on folding chairs: a man and a woman who looked like they'd been poured from instant professor packets — add Ph.D. and stir; and another Volkswagen bus of a woman in a sweat suit and cat glasses — her hair was two chopsticks in a bun. I shook their hands and smiled, I hoped, intelligently. Finished unraveling the scarf from my neck. Took a seat in the armchair thoughtfully reserved for me. They seemed edgy, but I just palmed it off as the awkward manners of university types who were more comfortable with books than people.

First thing, the professor-looking lady asked me how I would place my book in the Western tradition. I ignored my first impulse — rodeo boots and some cowgirl fringe — and said something about Charles Dickens and Edgar Allan Poe, hoping this wasn't one of those shows where they made fools of people with hidden cameras. I don't know how, but I could tell that the professor man and the sweat-suited lady couldn't stand each other. I guess it was the way one looked while the other was speaking. Once, while he was asking me about my experience, she pulled a chopstick from her hair and I thought for sure she was going to ram it into his heart; but she just chewed it thoughtfully, staring at him like she wished it were his liver.

I was doing pretty well here. They tossed out questions that I pretended to consider thoughtfully to buy time. Then I swatted back answers they pretended were fascinating. I'd never been on an interview for a real job before and it felt strangely like I was bargaining for my own life in a hostage situation.

Then, Chopsticks said, innocent as you please, "So, tell us about your teaching."

And just like that, I couldn't. What's strange is that this was the one question I'd anticipated, prepared for. But suddenly I could see the headlights of an anxiety attack bearing down on me, and in literal seconds, I was roadkill. I used to have about six anxiety attacks a day — no kidding — real

Godzillas, crushing me in their hands and hurling me against the walls. There'd be this roar in my ear, and everything would turn this horrible margarine yellow. My glands would leach every atom of moisture from my mouth and throat, drying them into sandpaper, and then spit it out of every pore as sweat. Worst of all, my heart became Muhammad Ali's fist, hammering at the door of my chest like Mrs. Ali was on the other side, fucking his best friend. My legs would go Gumby on me. I'd feel faint, my mind the aftermath of a pillow fight, all swirling feathers. During an anxiety attack, you're convinced you're going to die, but not before you lose your mind first. They're this weird dichotomy: on the inside, this cyclone rampages through you, bulleting telephone poles through barns, sweeping cows to the tops of the trees; outside, you're frozen.

Great.

I. Tried. To. Explain. How. I. Taught. I. Used. A. Book. Yes. A. Book. We. Read. The. Book. It. Was. A. Good. Book. I. Um. Read. Their. Stories. I. Um. Yes.

The man professor, who'd been tapping his pen on his knee, stopped, pen midair. The woman professor stared at me like I was slowly transforming into a giant praying mantis. Sweat Suit's mouth had dropped unpleasantly open and I could see her chopstick, resting on her tongue, chewed to a pulp. Which didn't help. Gibberish. Dear God, I was speaking gibberish.

Mercifully, I don't remember the rest of the interview. When anxiety attacks are done with you, they crumple you up and rim-shot you into the trash can. You just lie there with egg yolk on your cheek and coffee grounds in your hair, beyond caring. They said blah, blah, blah. I replied vacantly. They kept glancing down at their notes and conspicuously not cutting their eyes toward one another. The air was wadded with stale hotel heat. The Sahara of my mouth had reflooded, but it was too late.

I lugged my coat back on, flung my scarf around my neck, tried to smile, thanked them. The waitees down in the lobby were going to be hopping the next train to the tenure track. I could see that now. They were going to be on search committees and own foreign and expensive objects while I worked in a card shop, dusting the Hubbell figurines. Outside, it was still as misty and gray and sad as England under Thatcher. I decided that art might console me and headed for the Guggenheim.

Once there, I couldn't help but notice that everyone, and I mean everyone, was cruising me. The ticket taker, the coat-check girl, the security guards. Two Italian men, model material, the world was their runway, whispered in their liquid language and followed me through an exhibit of Russian constructivists. It was like some cosmic consolation prize. If I couldn't have worshipful graduate students and summers off, then at least I got to be sexy. I was going to wear this suit every day for the rest of my life.

I had a dinner date pretty early so I hurried away, unhappy to be leaving the new legions of my fans; but outside, it was the same Cinderella story. Doormen, rich young mothers trundling their children down the street in Cadillac strollers, the homeless. They couldn't keep their eyes off me. My cabby was so glued to his rearview mirror that he was running red lights and playing bumper cars against the curb. I checked my seat belt and gave him a little gift, one of my newly irresistible smiles. What did it hurt me? I was a cologne ad. I was Julia Roberts.

I couldn't wait to tell Ralph, though I probably wouldn't have to. He'd just swoon to the floor when he opened the door.

"What's that all over your face?" he asked, grimacing.

"What?" I said. So the carriage was a pumpkin after all.

"You'd better go have a look in the mirror."

And there go the glass slippers.

I was blue from the eyes down, and not pale blue either. I was Matisse blue, art-deco-glass blue, the flecks in the box of Tide blue. Safira, the schizophrenic lady on my block, would smear lipstick from the hairs of her nose to the ones on her chin to halfway across her cheeks. She thought it made her look pretty. That was me now, only in my case it seemed twice as nuts because my blue looked, exactly, like eye shadow, titty-dancer eye shadow. That gothic blue face hovering above that dull blue suit — Salvador Dalí couldn't have dreamed it up. Naturally, no one had said a word on the street because it looked deliberate — how could something like that not be deliberate — and you would not want to provoke the person who'd done it.

What the? How the? Where in the?

The scarf. Of course. The curse of the African scarf. That flea-bitten *shmata* of a scarf had bled in the mist. Oh, my interview. My poor, poor interview.

At my next Gotham class, we went over part of a novel Mai was working on. It was rambling and autobiographical and we were already familiar with many of the stories by the time we read them. The others were polite and tried to be helpful, though every time any of us made suggestions for improvement, Mai insisted that that's the way it had happened and she was sorry but to change even one word would have been felonious. The nice thing about going over Mai's story was that she wasn't supposed to talk, which she mostly stuck by, though there were moments when the springs of her practically spit from her sides and burst from her head like a cartoon clock.

Next was Tryphine. Her first chapter was poorly typed and often hard to follow. It was a South African epic with more characters than the last number of a Busby Berkeley movie; but it had strangulating descriptive passages of things like necklacing, which was when a tire was fitted around your throat and set fire to. It was almost impossible to reconcile the world of necklacing with the world of this children's classroom, with all its busy promise: a poster of how to make your cursive ABCs Scotch taped to the wall, the nubby fingers of the chalk. Speaking for myself, we all needed a long break to reel us back in.

Coffee. A cigarette. Melancholy. Ngong turned out to be the real writer, stories about a Catholic school she'd attended in Africa. They were like fairy tales in the blackness of their cruelty, but little bits of hope flickered here and there, like sparks whirling up from a bonfire into the night sky. Her sentences were limpid, but with muscular, almost alchemical evocations of landscape and character, with terrible ironies lashing through both.

There was some time left over, so I decided to read from the beginning of Carson McCullers's "The Ballad of the Sad Café" because I wanted to discuss landscape, character, and the terrible ironies lashing through both. What I had forgotten was my audience. What I had forgotten was this phrase: "It was such a night when it is good to hear from faraway, across the dark, the slow song of a Negro on his way to make love." As I began to read that sentence, as I heard the words "It was such a night . . ." I remembered, like a sudden bout of cramps, exactly where that sentence was speeding; and I tried to derail it, but in the chaos of trying to make it right, I ended up emphasizing "NEGRO." "NEGRO," I said, expectorating the word, achoo, violently sneezing it out.

Dear God.

By the time Miss Amelia's Cousin Lymon arrived at the end of the paragraph, ball bearings of sweat slithered down my sides. I looked up, expecting to see the tiny gang of my students biting pirates' knives between their teeth. Fred was placid, his fingers laced over his belly. Mai was examining her fingernails like they were a code she had to break. Tryphine seemed lost deep in thought. Ngong, the real writer, looked amused, like what a funny little man I was, what a hobbit of a fellow.

No one said a word. Fortunately, class was over.

Afterward, Fred said he wanted to write a story about a guy who went back to the Midwest to visit. He said it was really weird. I decided to trust him on that and encouraged him to go for it. Mai told me the entire rest of her novel. It was like being slowly filled with beeswax. I kept saying things like, uh-huh, no kidding, really? Tryphine asked me if I thought her novel was worth writing. I told her if people were fitting tires around one another's necks and setting fire to them, then she had a duty to report it. Ngong waited. She let the others wander away. I pushed my stuff into the open mouth of my backpack, smiled at her. She smiled back, and her smile felt like that brown stuff they rub on you in surgery before they cut you open and yank out your liver. We made small talk. Hers was like the Romanov jeweled box of small talk. Mine was like that same box, except that it had been made in Taiwan and bought in Atlantic City.

In the elevator, she said, "What was that novel you read from again?"

"Uh, it was from a novella, 'The Ballad of the Sad Café,' by Carson McCullers."

"It was very . . . beautiful. I think I could learn something from that."

"Yes, well, you're both writing something that's more . . . talelike."

"Exactly."

"Here," I said, scrambling through my pack as the elevator doors creaked slowly open like they were haunted.

"Thank you," she said. "I will read it this week." Then she gave me a smile that was as slow as six deliberate paper cuts. "You can still learn from a woman who says 'Negro.'"

One night when I got home, Becky was in John's spot on the couch, her head thrown back and at an angle like she'd broken her neck. Pillars of boxes labeled CHRISTMAS stood around like the last few guests at a party. She lifted her head and a ninety-eight-pound weakling of a smile limped across her face. "John's back in the hospital."

"I'm sorry."

"He's not going to be coming back out."

"Oh, Becky."

The terrible silence of two people who didn't know what to say next. Becky very deliberately brightened her smile. There was something desperately managerial about it, maybe something she'd picked up from a positive-thinking seminar and now couldn't get rid of. Who knows? Maybe it worked.

"I was supposed to go back tomorrow," Becky said.

"I can keep an eye on him if you want."

"That's sweet, but my parents are coming up on Sunday."

"Good."

She looked past me. "He said he was fine."

"Yeah, well. I guess it's a hard thing to admit. To yourself. To anyone."

"He wore himself out trying to show me the city. I wish I'd come sooner."

"You didn't know."

"I mean sooner. More times. He's going and . . . I haven't seen him enough." There were enough cobwebs in her voice at the end of that sentence for a whole block of haunted houses.

"Hey. I have an idea. Why don't we have dinner tonight?" I suppose that was a nice idea, but it also made me flutteringly uncomfortable because it seemed shallow somehow. I checked my back to make sure Martha Stewart's ventriloquist hand wasn't shoved in there.

"I get back from the hospital at about nine. Is that too late?"

"Not in the city that never sleeps." When exactly had my mind been destroyed? Next thing you know I'd be calling it the Big Apple, Gotham. But then I remembered that death — the primitive, stone face of it — made you stupid.

That night we met at the little Indian place around the corner, which was more of a hallway than a restaurant. Red fabric, geometrically patterned in mirrors, served as a kind of wallpaper and was also swagged from the ceiling. It had the cozy feeling of a child's fort. There was a pleasant hum in the curry-fragrant air.

Becky told me she lived . . . somewhere. I can't really remember, but it was the sort of place where you could own a bed-and-breakfast that catered to the championship fishermen who frequented the nearby lake, which was exactly what she and her husband did. They'd both been wildly successful at bank marketing technologies, something. About five years ago they'd decided they'd had it. Cashed in the stocks, sold the house. It was a Horatio Alger story for the nineties.

"Great," I said. I only half meant it. I had a lifelong aversion to fishing. My father had taken me once as a child, and I'd badgered him the whole time. Was he sure the hooks didn't hurt in the fishes' mouths? Because they sure looked like they did. When I found out we had to slit them in half and scoop their guts out with our bare hands, I locked myself in the car. With the car keys. I knew getting gouged open hurt, and I felt betrayed, because now I suspected the hooks hurt too. I sat there in the driver's seat stubbornly, my face locked in a frown, my arms twisted tightly around my chest, staring straight ahead as my father pounded the window and yelled versions of "Open this damn car door, or else." I finally caved, but not before he promised a) not to beat the living daylights out of me, and b) not to ever make me fish again. My father was a relatively honorable man, and to his credit he stuck by his word.

Becky fascinated me because in the places where I was filled with dread, she was filled with zeal. She could easily have been the host of one of those late-night infomercials where you buy things for no money down and then sell them for a colossal profit. I faked being an upbeat guy myself, figuring there was no point in subjecting a stranger with that kind of drill sergeant's determination to be happy to my own morbid personality, particularly when her brother was dying. So when she asked about me, and she did so pointedly, at regular intervals, with the nodding, interested gaze of a therapist, I spun it. No one who knew me would have recognized my life. I had all the facts right, but every miserable failure had become an opportunity. Things were *grreeaatt!* If you called now you also got a desk set, valued at more than one hundred dollars.

But around dessert — a tasteless, odorless, textureless flan — it began to unravel. She began to unravel. It was hard owning your own business. To tell the truth, she'd never worked so hard in her life. And it wasn't as profitable as I might think. There were some months when she was borrowing from Peter to pay Paul. And the winding melancholy of that set her on the road to John. He'd always been a special little boy, very bright, and she wasn't just saying that because he was her brother either. His teachers had all said so too. He'd won things in school, for penmanship, perfect attendance. But he'd had a tough time finding his way. When he'd finally become an RN, about the time she'd gotten the bed-and-breakfast, she'd been so happy. She'd always known that there was something special he'd been meant to do. He'd loved it so much, he'd been so good at it, he'd finally found his life. You would have thought their parents would have been a little more . . . accepting.

Oh, it wasn't just John and his, lifestyle. There was that, but believe you me they hadn't been any easier on her, not one bit. Her mother was so critical, and here her mother had been an alcoholic. Oh, she wouldn't admit to being a drunk, and she didn't drink anymore. But she had been one, and when she drank, she'd been mean. Nasty. Why couldn't Becky stick to a diet? She'd never get a man looking like that. And then when Becky did land one, married him, well it was, oh sure, him, who couldn't have gotten that? And did she get an ounce of credit for being so well-off, owning her business? No, she didn't. It was all about why couldn't she have any grand-children. Well, she couldn't have children, but did her mother care about that? No, she didn't. Don't get her wrong, she loved her mother, she really did, but Mom was as hard a woman as ever drew breath.

My own family wasn't exactly the von Trapps, and I dragged out a few of my choicer war stories in sympathy. It was funny listening to Becky sing the song, every verse, of the whole John. I'd only known him as the person he'd finally become; and it was final because there was no time left to become again. He'd never have the chance to quit smoking, buy some yoga tapes, sign up for those drawing classes he'd always meant to take. He wouldn't be getting around to any-thing anymore. He'd never fall in love with a set dresser and move to Los Angeles. He'd already had the great love of his life, whoever that was. Now all he could do was struggle to keep the person he was alive.

But he had been a child — Becky had said something about being forced to play Little League — and then he'd been an adolescent, maybe taking the girl he'd been best friends with since second grade to the prom, with all the usual pictures on a fairyland prom bridge. He'd been a young man in New York, diverted by the easy promises the city could keep, his heart busy with ones it couldn't. He'd dropped out of college and moved in with Buddy and then he'd become a nurse. It wasn't easy to become a nurse. That human life was being wrenched away from him. I could see it now, his particular absence, swimming there in his sister's eyes.

The next afternoon, a Saturday, I went to look at another apartment on the Upper West Side in the midnineties. This was a relatively good deal, six-fifty a month, but it didn't include anything. The neighborhood was a mixture of SROs and older people wheeling groceries around in wobbly carts. The man's name was Guy — rhymes with "spree" — DeVille. Cruella's brother. Guy was probably in his sixties, though he could have been in his fifties or his seventies. He was squat, but ominously well preserved.

He opened the door with a subdued, undertaker's smile. "Wesley?"

"Guy?" He'd already corrected my pronunciation on the phone.

I followed him down a cavernous hall so dark you couldn't see the bats hanging from the ceiling. Huge, framed posters seemed to cover the wall to my left, but that's only a guess. We turned into a drawing room, that's the only thing you could possibly call it. The ceiling was tented in pleated, green satin. A chandelier the size of Versailles hung from it. The furniture was baroque, and a small nation of china figurines bowing at violins and curtsying and doing minuets capered across the various marble tabletops and mantels-for-no-good-reason. Gilt everywhere. A pop-eyed pug was drooling on a settee flocked in green velvet.

Guy himself was dressed as an ordinary man in a short-sleeved shirt, Ban-Lon pants, and loafers. He sat down beside the pug, put her in his lap, and began stroking her, a gesture I was almost certain he'd copied from Morticia Addams with one of her pet spiders. "This is Gigi," he said.

"Hello there," I said, bending toward Gigi. She turned her head from me, ostentatiously. I hadn't known that dogs felt human emotions, like disdain.

"Have a seat."

I did, on a Louis XIV chair in the same flocked velvet, so spindly it looked like it would splinter under me. "This is quite a place you got here."

He shrugged. It was nothing. "So, tell me about yourself, Wesley."

He'd put the quarter in. He'd pulled the lever. But this time, in addition to the usual dim palette of responsibility I painted from, I added a few bright colors that made me sound perhaps a tad too civilized for this mortal coil, not unlike Guy himself. He nodded approvingly. Yes, our mutual sophistication was a burden.

"Well," he said, "that all sounds splendid. This Gay Roommating Service thing." Mock shudder. "You wouldn't believe some of the types that have paraded through here."

"Yeah, you wouldn't believe some of the places I've looked at."

"No doubt. Would you like to see the rest of the apartment?"

He kept Gigi in his arms. Decent kitchen. A bathroom lit by candles spinning Norma Desmond shadows across the royal-blue walls. My bedroom was neither here nor there, but it was sizable enough. A window with a fire escape, where I could imagine sitting in spring, with a gin and tonic, after Telesessions. Except for a certain mausoleum musk, and even that had its appeal, it looked like a good gig. We retired back to the drawing room.

"So, Wesley, do you think you could live . . . here?" He waved a hand at his humble splendor.

"I think I could, Guy."

"I suppose we should both think about it for a day or so. My dear friend, Alicia Alonso, used to say it was never a good idea to rush into anything. Not that she ever heeded her own advice."

"Alicia Alonso, the dancer?"

"Is there another?"

"Wow." I'm almost embarrassed to admit how impressed I really was.

"You don't get to be my age without meeting a few people." He tickled Gigi's nose. She snorted. Keys clattered in a door and then footsteps creaked down the haunted hall. "Oh dear," Guy said.

Ax murderer? No, just a man in a hip-hop sweat suit with pockmarked, peanut-butter-colored skin and white, spiky hair. He sort of fell against the doorframe. It was hard to tell his age too. Anywhere from twenty-five to forty-five. Whatever it was, there'd been heavy mileage over mountainous terrain. His eyes were bloodshot and the vodka on his breath insecticided the room.

"Mario," Guy said. Duchess-at-tea posture. "Aren't you supposed to be at school?"

"We got out early," he slurred, and made his way to the cocktail cart with the slow, steady precision of a drunk keeping his balance. Guy closed his eyes in disgust. Gigi's loose skin oozed up between his fingers. You could tell she wanted to hop down and start licking Mario's sweat suit as he slopped gin into a crystal goblet, and had a gulp.

"Mario stays with me sometimes," Guy said. Rictus of a smile.

"Yeah, hey, don't worry," Mario said. "It's not like I live here or anything like that. You know. Just a flop sometimes."

"It's a bit more than a flop, Mario." Guy raised his eyebrows at me. I smiled understandingly.

"I don't know about this air-conditioning-repair school," Mario said. "It's like, you know, it's gonna interfere with my music. My music, man."

"Your music?" Guy said. His tone could have poisoned a tristate area.

"Yeah, my music. My. Music. My dad's the greatest fucking guitarist in Panama."

"Mario, we've been all through the career of your illustrious father — in Panama — a number of times."

"Yeah, well, he's played all over the world. Not just Panama."

Guy rolled his eyes so far back in his head I thought he'd bruise his corneas. "My manners. Wesley, this is Mario. Mario, Wesley."

Mario, forgetting to concentrate on walking, staggered a bit on the way over to shake my hand. I stood up. He pumped my arm like oil might spout from my mouth. "Hey, man. Nice to meet you. So you here looking at the room?"

"Yeah."

"Great place, huh?"

"Terrific."

"Guy's really into antiques. This stuff's the real deal, not the cheap shit."

I could feel Guy wincing over Mario's shoulder. "It certainly looks it," I said.

"Wanna drink?"

"No thanks."

"It's a little early for me too, but hey. Weekend."

Guy stepped between us, Gigi cradled in his arms. She leaned over to lick Mario's drink. Snorted. "See," Mario said, "even Gigi likes a little drink. Nothing wrong with that."

"I'm sure Wesley's a very busy young man," Guy said. "I'm sure he doesn't really have time for all . . . this."

"I probably should be going," I said.

"OK," Mario said, reaching around Guy to clap me on the shoulder. "Great to meet you, man. Maybe we'll be seeing you around."

"I hope so."

Guy let Gigi down. She waddled over to the door, looked up at us expectantly. "She thinks it's time for her W-A-L-K," Guy said, smiling. She was a naughty girl. Demanding, but lovable.

Gigi tapped along beside us down the hall, me pressing like

a mime against the dark to make sure I didn't smack into a wall. Guy said, low, "I hope Mario won't influence your decision."

"No," I said, same decibels, "he seemed. Charming."

Guy made a sound in his throat. "You haven't known very many charming people, have you, Wesley?"

"When you get to be my age, you've met a few."

At the door, he said, "Well, I hope this will work out for both of us."

"Me too."

I was in, and I felt OK about it, not great. But I supposed that Guy and his ilk were my fate, the ones who had sort of wandered out of time. My life had always been populated by hopeless eccentrics, derelicts and losers, like some Leonard Cohen song. As a little boy, the suburbs had seemed like a sinister Disneyland. The air fresheners and the spray cheeses had all seemed pretend to me, probably because I couldn't get the simplest little-boy thing right, not Little League, not Hot Wheels, not fistfights. What was happening inside me had nothing to do with what was happening outside me, which was what appeared to be happening to everybody else. What had made me sad, as a child, was that I knew that people died in this pretend world, which made it not pretend at all. And that's why I'd gotten religion — I'd wanted it all to solidify into someplace where you died and then it meant something. That never happened.

But several years later, as I pushed through the pages of a magazine, I ran across a big spread about pop art. There was a collage, and though I didn't quite understand what that was, I couldn't stop watching it: a muscle-man dad sporting a giant Tootsie Pop that even I could see was meant to be his dick; a glamour-puss of a mom in black underwear and sunglasses; the house a jumble of products, and that was the thing, I could see they were meant to be the things I saw advertised on TV. The picture was called *Just What Is It That Makes Today's Homes so Modern, so Appealing . . . ?* And I laughed this disbelieving laughter I had never laughed before. It was a storm breaking through and flushing away one of those horrible, humid Virginia days, flooding everything with cool breathable air. So, there *were* other people out there like me. All I had to do now was find those people when I grew up. At any cost.

Becky left a nice note. Late Sunday night the parents arrived. I didn't see much of them. They were basically camped at the hospital.

On Wednesday night Telesessions ended early because one of the conferences had crashed and burned. That happened sometimes. You called the docs and nobody was home. I got in at about 9:00, and John's parents, instead of snoring under their home-brought blankets on the foldout, were huddled over slices of pizza at the dining-room table. It was the first time I'd gotten a good look at them. Mom had a little shrub of tight, gray curls, those big, eighties-style glasses. She wore sweaters and her skin had an Oil of Olay sheen. Dad had a comb-over and dressed like a golfer. His ears were enormous, stuck straight out like shutters, and the light showed pink through them, highlighting the discreet fur collar around their edges.

"Hey there, Wes," Dad said. "Care to join us here for a little slice of pizza?"

"Thanks. No. It takes me a little while to work up to food."

"You need to eat," Mom said, though she'd had about one bite of her own pizza and was now smoking. I could tell she was one of those women who basically lived off coffee and spite.

"How's about a little drink?" He waggled ginger ale and something at me. It looked like a urine test, with possibly bad results, but I figured I'd choked down worse.

"Sure, that would be nice."

He pushed back his chair to go get it, but Mom said, "I'll do it," wearily crushing her cigarette out. "I don't drink anymore," she said to me.

"Yeah," I said, not thinking. "Becky said something about that."

She gave her husband a look, like how many times have I told you about that girl, and said, "I'm sure."

He didn't look up from his pizza.

From the kitchen, the sounds of her making the drink, loud. The smell of the pizza was comforting, so normal somehow, like next we'd be playing Parcheesi while the World Series played in the background. I shrugged off my backpack, wondered where I should sit. It seemed impolite to sit at the table while they were eating. The living room felt too far away.

Mom handed me my drink, sternly. I ended up pulling out a chair and joined them at the table. Dad chewed. Mom lit another cigarette. Ginger ale and bourbon. That's what the drink was. It was way too sweet, like something a drunken brunette would cadge from a horny businessman. I lit a cigarette to take the edge off and Mom pushed the ashtray toward me.

"So John tells us you're a writer," Dad said.

Oh God, not that. When people said that, they meant something else. They meant that you effortlessly pirouetted to your desk, and then you transcribed all the important events of your life, you made it deep and moving and then Dino DeLaurentis bought the movie rights after discussing it with his wife, Sophia Loren, who might play you. What it meant to me was that I dragged myself to my desk, chewed my fingers to the bloody stumps of my knuckles, tried this, despaired, tried another phrase or word or maybe I needed to switch this to the third person, blah, blah, blah, blah, blah. It felt, except for certain occasions of mysterious inspiration, like back-breaking work, and that made me feel guilty because I came from a family where I knew what backbreaking work really felt like, and I wasn't working in a coal mine, so what the fuck was I complaining about?

So there was a certain admiration to Dad's simple state-ment that felt false, and I winced, smiling, but I winced. I wanted to try to explain what it really meant, for me, but I was, unfortunately, way too inarticulate on the best days, and now I was tired from Telesessions, and weirded out because they were his parents, and their son was dying, and I didn't even know him, and yet here I was. But that conversation seemed so much more complicated that I didn't even know where to begin. Besides, he was just making polite conversation, and I was sane enough, or at least mannerly enough, to realize that.

"Yeah. Sort of. I don't know."

"What's your book about?"

"Uh. A family."

"Sounds interesting."

"Hm, I hope so. It didn't do very well."

"So how'd you get to be a writer?" Mom asked.

"I'm not really sure." I thought about that. "It seems like I just kept doing it until somebody finally published me. So what do you guys do?"

"Well, John Sr. here's retired from the military."

"My dad was in the Air Force."

"How long?" John Sr. asked.

"Thirty-some years," I said.

"The service is a good life."

"He seemed to like it."

"So you're an Army brat."

"Little bit. My parents got divorced when I was pretty young."

Silence. Mom rubbed the small of her back and winced. Dad wiped around his mouth with a paper towel and patted his stomach, which was flat. Military man. The liquid candy of my drink burned. I sat there smiling at nothing in particular because there was nothing in particular to smile about, but I couldn't think of anything else to do with my face. Mom didn't worry about it. She just scowled, like everything was bound to be a disappointment in the long run, so why should we kid ourselves? Maybe she was right.

"Uh, Wes," John Sr. said, stretching. Mom cleared their plates and picked up the pizza box. "You need to get straight with Becky about the rent."

"You know, actually, John has my deposit."

He held up his hand. "I don't know nothing about that. That's between you and John. All's I know is that Becky's took care of November and you boys need to get right with her."

"Why don't you just keep my part of it when you get the deposit back?"

He cracked his knuckles. From the kitchen, the silent sounds of eavesdropping. "I don't know that there's gonna be any deposit."

"Why not?"

"Just things. With John. To tell you the truth we're damn lucky the landlord's letting us have November. He coulda throwed the lot of us out on our ass. You boys just need to get right with Becky and that's all there is to it."

The way I saw it, I was being cheated out of about two thousand dollars. The way they'd see it, I would have cheated them out of about seven hundred when the dust from John's grave finally cleared. My deposit would have paid November's rent twice. As it was I was going to have to beg, borrow, and blow my way into Guy's.

Sorry. No could do. But I slapped on my poker face and said, "When's Becky coming back?"

"Early next week."

"I'll get right with her then." Shameless. I really didn't want to screw Becky that way, especially since I knew she got fucked plenty in this family; but I couldn't face duking out my last few weeks here over who owed what to whom.

"Okeydokey," he said, slapping the table. From the kitchen, the sudden sounds of dishes being washed. "Mother, you just about ready to make the bed?"

"*Law and Order*'s coming on."

"We got us another big day tomorrow."

"That's my favorite show," she said.

He rubbed his eyes, deeply, and shook his head. "Well, fix me another drink then. You want one, Wes?"

"No thanks. I might step out for a while."

From the kitchen — "You best be careful going out there all hours. I wish John hadda been more careful. I don't know why, you people, have to go and live in New York and everything else. John coulda had a good life. You just don't know what this is like on your poor mothers. You don't."

On Thursday Alan told me that his boyfriend had found him a place out in Queens. He also had no intention of handing a red cent over to Becky, partially because of the deposit, but also because he was only going to be there a couple more weeks. He was going to string her along too, he said without a flinch of conscience. What had seemed so reasonable when I'd thought it through sounded petty and surly and small in his mouth. I could see now how scrabbling through life could turn you into an Alan. You weren't really trying to hurt anyone. You were just taking care of number one because there wasn't another living soul there to do it for you. I felt like I'd slunk past some invisible border where I might find myself knocking down little old ladies for their purses, telling myself I needed the cash more than they did because they were going to die soon anyway. I'd always thought of myself as a fairly decent person; but now I had to shake hands with the fact that under the right circumstances I could have turned out to be anybody.

It was officially November, officially cold. Central Park had gone on its winter diet, but still managed to have an odd, gray, strangulated beauty. The neighborhood grocery store was filled with butternut squash and crepe-paper turkeys that opened like books. The squash was cheap and I bought a lot of it, because with butter it was dinner; with honey, dessert. I was trying not to spend a dime, which was laughable. The price of cigarettes seemed to go up hourly.

John's parents left, and I told them I'd look in on John, which I did. The usual horror story of the end was near. I didn't know why we had to die, so savagely, and in such fear. I really didn't. The machines, tucked into him, did their mindless jobs with infuriating assurance. The sun was out there, burning and burning and burning, bathing the room in a milk of light; outside, making chlorophyll and evaporation and carrots; outside, making everything. In fact, the nurse down the hall was eating carrots she'd brought in a Ziploc bag. She'd been flipping the pages of her clipboard and the edges of her mouth were stained orange. That was her life, trickling away. She'd never remember that carotened moment; I'd never forget it. We just went along, one thing after the other, wiping out an ashtray with a paper towel, having our hearts wrung like dishcloths.

John farted, so much for death with dignity; but then he opened his eyes, smiled at me, and reached for my hand. His skin was papery and warm. The bones of his fingers were as sharp as broken Bic pens.

"Buddy?" he said.

"No. Wesley."

"Oh." His eyes drifted back shut. "Buddy must have just left."

"Must have."

"Have you seen my jeans?" he asked lazily.

"I don't think so."

"The ones with the rip in the knee and no back pocket?"

"Oh yeah," I lied. "I think I saw them back home."

His head lolled to the side. "They make my ass look nice."

"I'll see if I can't find them the next time I come."

"I hope Carmine didn't pee on them."

Carmine? "Hmmm . . . I'm sure Carmine wouldn't do a thing like that."

"I don't know. She's a very bad cat. I told and told and told Buddy about her. But he loves her."

"What are you gonna do with a guy like that?"

"I don't know why we come here anyway. It's so hot and smoky."

"But oo-la-la, the men."

"No fats, no fems."

And with that, his grip went limp.

A couple of days later, he died.

Jo Ann came to see me my last couple of days in the apartment. I was grateful because it was all packed up and echoey. All these things were waiting, unbearably, to be dumped off at the Salvation Army, and then to be scattered into lives where their exact meanings would be blurred. John's dreamcatcher on a guest-bathroom wall, a poor place to catch dreams. During the good hours, I imagined that his Johnness would still cling to his crystal wizards somehow, like a scent. But mostly it just felt like some final abandonment; except a brother, who showed up at the very end, did take the giant TV. Those crazy people who preserved the rooms of their dead, the sachet just so on the vanity, the dried willows on the sill, all the Mrs. Havishams of this world, how well I came to understand them in those final days. Maybe the Egyptians had been right: you should take it with you.

John's parents had asked me if I'd wanted anything, and in truth, I didn't; but I said that I really liked that one drawing, one of a futuristic city, because I wanted them to think that even though they didn't understand it, or him, some of us had thought he was a neat guy with cool stuff. I was thinking of myself, of course. My mother or sister or brother shaking their heads sorrowfully over the baffling — to them — choices of my own life, and packing them up, not even bothering with newspaper so my Barbie Christmas ornaments wouldn't lose an arm or a sliver of ball gown or a chip of their ponytailed hair. I didn't want my Barbies on some lady's tree — a lady who'd picked them up at the Salvation Army and couldn't see that they were both pretty *and* funny.

So I took the drawing, even though it was flat and proportionless, even though the future didn't look like much of one. John said a friend of his who'd gone to art school had given it to him. I lifted it from the wall and I said, too heartily, "I always liked this." Stretching out my arms, I eyeballed it, nodding, like, yeah, this is really something; and his mother said, tentatively, but trying, perhaps, for one flickering moment, to understand her son's life, "Yes, I can see how a person might like that." Then she shook the thought from her head the way a dog tries to shake off water and said, "Of course it wouldn't go with anything in my house."

Of course.

So it sat askew on top of my own boxed-up belongings, and Jo Ann had said she thought she could collage some pictures into it, things John would like — a space helmet, candles, maybe a tiny velvet Jesus (no Jesus, I said quickly) — that might also make it nice for me to look at. I liked that idea, of our lives being pasted together, John's and mine, the layers of what he had cherished overlapping with the layers of what I still did. It seemed like a fitting inheritance for a world where friends were family, and family were strangers, and you might find yourself helping someone else to die because you'd been yoked to them by accidents of commerce and the mysterious trick of your own sexual nature and some fumbling attempt at compassion.

Jo Ann and I went to a neighborhood diner for lunch because it was cheap, in theory. But between the seven-dollar tuna melts and the three-dollar Cokes and the jewel-encrusted fries, we may as well have gone to Tres Chez Nosegay for Château Margaux and *fruits de mer*. Also, it wasn't really a pretty place. It looked like it had been redone in the eighties, based on the evil pink floral prints of Laura Ashley. I couldn't stop thinking: shoulder pads. I'll say this for it, it sure did gleam. This was the Upper East Side, so there were a lot of older ladies having the $1.95 cup of vegetable soup with crackers *and* bread, their far-from-new shopping bags filled with God knows what tucked by their hips.

"I don't know how you stand to live here," Jo Ann said. We couldn't smoke, but you could tell that her hands, though they were perfectly still, were restless to do just that.

"I like it when you go into the subway and there's this unbelievable Chinese violinist playing Mozart for quarters."

"OK, in the first place it's sad that he's only playing for quarters. And in the second, how do you even know it's Mozart? You didn't even know the 'Kill-the-Wabbit' song was a real classical song."

"OK. So maybe it's Chopin."

"Look, you can't even get a decent Coke in this town. Have you tasted yours?"

"OK, what about this? I like looking at the Vermeers at the Met. I've been, like, six times to see them. I could look at them every day for the rest of my life."

"I know. It's just this whole tuna-melt thing. What's it going to come with, a side of Elizabeth Taylor's diamond necklaces?"

"I was hoping it came with a blow job until I got a load of the waiter."

"I don't think we should be talking about blow jobs in the middle of all this pink vinyl. I feel like I'm inside Chatty Cathy and she's listening."

The waiter, a Greek guy with a mop of black curls, a belly he was working on, and one technologically advanced pair of Nikes, brought us platters of tuna melt the size of satellite dishes. Two great pyramids of potato chips. Two dill pickles like martian canoes. The fries could have fed the block.

"Hot," he said.

"I'm full just looking at this," Jo Ann said.

"I'm having full-blown nausea."

Still, we nibbled at the slabs of tuna melt, picked at the fries. A gooey version of Billy Joel's "Uptown Girl" was caramelizing the air. Suddenly this image of John sitting in here, the billboard of the menu unfurled before him, considering the atomic colors of the BLT photograph, hit me like a seizure. I thought I was going to cry. There was no reason to hide anything from Jo Ann, but I didn't want to cry over the punk-rock green of the dill pickles.

"Hey," I said, to whack it out of me, "here's some good news."

"Really?"

"This girl I'm teaching, Ngong, she's really talented."

"What a musical name."

"And I think she's actually learning something from me. She turned in a revision this week and it was like, she got it."

"That's practically a miracle."

The lady beside us dumped her plastic basket of cellophaned crackers into her shopping bag, and over by the cash register the waiters were muttering in Greek. I could hardly stand the thought of them throwing out our potato chips — there was enough for a $1.99 bag, and I wanted a cigarette. But I was OK. You thought you were going because your own life had you by the throat, was throttling the last breath out of you; and you wanted to plug in, recharge, find your way back to the only thing you'd ever been good at. For me, that happened to be writing. Then you got there and it seemed like you were supposed to save somebody else's life: how noble, how bold. But it turned out you couldn't save anyone's life, not even your own in the long run. Still. You could point Ngong in the direction of her voice, and you could lug Mr. McNally from the toilet when you had to. Friends like Jo Ann were there to hoist you back up and dust you back off and get some fluids into you. Help was possible and necessary and true.

"You know," I said, "I've always wanted to end a story just with 'I love you.'"

"That would be difficult."

"That's why I'd like to try it."

"I don't know, that has huge ick potential."

"OK, what if it wasn't the very end? What if it was just like, close to the end?"

"You know, all I can see here is Ali MacGraw on her deathbed."

"I love you, Preppie," I said wanly, clutching my fork to my breast and dewing coleslaw juice on the collar of my sweater.

Jo Ann rolled her eyes. "Here's an ending for you. Two people are sitting in a diner, and one of them shrugs his shoulders and says, 'I don't know.'"

Shrugging my shoulders, I said, "I don't know."

Acknowledgments

I'd like to thank the following people, who read this manuscript in one form or another and offered some sort of help or advice in its making and publication. The Sunday Boys' Club: David Groff, Charles Flowers, Jim Currier, Will Berger. Also: Jose Garcia, Ralph Sassone, Rochelle Feinstein, Michael Pietsch, Asya Muchnick. And finally: Jo Ann Beard, who suggested that I write it, and then listened to almost every word, as I wrote it, over the phone.

You Are Here

A Memoir of Arrival

by Wesley Gibson

A READING GROUP GUIDE

A conversation
with Wesley Gibson

What made you decide to write this book? Of all the parts of your life you might have written about, what made you choose to focus on this particular story?

The truth is that I had finished a draft of a novel, but I wasn't ready to go back and rewrite it. But I wanted to be writing and I wasn't feeling particularly inspired. I was talking to Jo Ann at one point, and she said, "Why don't you write about your experience with John, because you've always been kind of haunted by it." I had been, and I had also felt there were other meanings in that experience besides my own personal grief.

At first I was going to write a thirty-page essay. But when I began, I found myself thinking, "To talk about this, I also have to bring up this . . ." and after working on it for a long time — over the course of a couple of years — the manuscript had become a few hundred pages.

It felt to me that there were many meanings here. One hundred years ago, most people didn't leave their little towns and died in the bosom of their families. It seemed to me that this contemporary story represented a pretty large social revision. A hundred years ago, what happened to John, and the way it happened, was a fairly impossible scenario. I wanted to describe it and to tease the meanings from it.

Of course, this situation might seem in some ways singular, but, in fact, because of AIDS there were lots of people helping strangers die, and somehow that was widening our sense of social responsibility. I don't think it's a specifically gay experience. I have straight friends who are estranged from their families, or whose parents are dead, and who depend on their friends to help them through difficult times. But the gay experience is at least partly where this story sprang from: that we feel obligated to people we don't have a blood attachment with.

You make a point in You Are Here *about friends taking the place of family in our culture, and family seeming more like strangers. Yet family also seems to play a crucial role in the book. Do you feel your own family has had a strong influence on you?*

Of course those people influence you. They're the ones who shape you, for good or for ill. To use the example in my book, I guess I learned very early on this peculiar thing about family: On the one hand, with my father's family, there was this enveloping love you were stitched into. But as I began to realize my profound difference from these people, I also began to realize how accidental that was.

My family showed me the possibility of what it felt like to be part of a group that nourished you and accepted you in a world where people are making judgments about one another all the time. Not that they weren't making judgments, but they would accept you no matter what. I think that experience is profoundly important to one's sense of stability in the world.

But as you get older, it becomes clear how much you're not like the rest of your family, especially if they are all like one another. It starts to feel like you've been beamed in from Saturn. They accept you, but there's an isolation there. Still, once you get a taste of that belonging as a child, you want to re-create it.

Some re-create it in their own families: they get married and have kids. But since that wasn't an option for me — not to say that gay people don't bond or connect as committed couples, or adopt or have children — I unconsciously began to form my own family through my friends. Of course, the role Jo Ann plays in the book is emblematic of that. Jo Ann was not my only friend in New York at the time, but she represents the kind of friendships I've woven together to make a family.

In other ways too I've learned a great deal from my family. My mother taught me independence. Coming from a working-class family also gives you a very good bullshit detector. It makes you intolerant of a certain kind of pretension, and I'm grateful for that.

My imagination and what storytelling ability I have I got from my grandmother and my aunts. As I wrote in the book, while I was growing up, a huge part of what the women in my family did was tell stories, all the time, and I'd sort of curl up at their feet and listen to them.

Naturally, I got bad things from my family too. As kids, we weren't encouraged to think too highly of ourselves. We were soundly slapped down for being too big for our britches, and that doesn't exactly inspire self-confidence.

So, of course, the family is the great cauldron where we're all brewed.

In writing a memoir, you've depicted real people, some of whom may actually read your book. Did you feel any desire to be less candid, or more candid, given the thought that some of your "characters" may pick up the book and recognize themselves in its pages?

I tried to be as truthful as I possibly could be. I figured if I was going to do it, I would have to be honest because otherwise, what's the point?

I was never worried I would make someone out to be villainous, because people are complicated. There are certainly wicked people in the world, but 99 percent of us fall into the gray area. I wasn't writing about wicked people but about the gray area, which includes myself.

Certainly there were a couple of moments that gave me pause. I was concerned about my mother reading this book. I was concerned about being candid about myself because I don't really talk about these things with my mother. I don't think anybody does. So when I found out the book was coming out, I called her and told her, "There's stuff in this book that I'm not sure you want to know about me. I wouldn't want to know it about you." And she said, "OK." And I don't think she's going to read it.

The family I describe on my father's side — they're probably going to be pretty appalled when they read this book. It's too frank for them, the gay stuff alone. They bought my novel when it came out and they read it, out of a sense of duty, I think. But they basically thought it was a piece of filth.

I tried to be honest about my own dark moments in the book. There are moments of realization when I see that I could have been anybody, and the fact that I may end up doing the right thing instead of the wrong thing is as much a result of circumstance as anything. But in terms of my credibility, I feel that I have to show the more shadowy parts of my character. Like most people, I'm trying to do the right thing — and often failing miserably at it. But trying.

Are there any stories from your experience in New York around this time that didn't make it into the book?

So many. Well, I did end up moving in with Guy De Ville, and that was its own little saga. He would come home on Friday nights with a grocery bag of vodka and would disappear into the bedroom with Mario, and I wouldn't see them again until Sunday afternoon, when he came out to make shepherd's pie. And the apartment had this terrible roach problem, so I would come into the kitchen and turn on the lights, and the shepherd's pie would be vibrating with roaches.

Before that, when I was still looking at apartments, there was one guy who opened the door wearing a leather cap and leather pants that were unbuttoned. Nothing else. And he laid back on this couch while he talked to me, legs spread. I don't think he even had a room to rent.

But I guess mostly in writing the book I tried to stick to the narrative thread. Or maybe the meaning thread. I dated someone during this time, and initially I wrote some scenes about that which were actually pretty funny. But when I looked at the whole book, I couldn't figure out the narrative importance of those sections. It wasn't clear how they fit into the puzzle of the book, because this wasn't a book about my love life, necessarily. So I took those scenes out.

Is it important to you that the book be considered within the canon of gay memoir, or gay literature? Or rather that it be seen apart from these categories?

Sure, I'd love to be part of the gay canon. There are some pretty great books in there. But I resist categorization because I think it's reductive, absurd, and ultimately crippling: "You're gay and so you can't do this. You're gay and so this is true about you." There was a time when it was more useful to talk about women's writing or gay writing; and I still think it's probably useful in the way it is to examine literature from a Marxist perspective or, say, in discerning certain strains in American literature. But for me that's a scholarly project and I am definitely not a scholar.

I can't imagine writers thinking of themselves in terms of categories when they're doing their work. I also think things have changed. David Sedaris and Michael Cunningham are on the bestseller list and no one really talks about them as specifically gay writers. I think that's a good thing. Another example: Does anyone really think of Alice Munro as a woman writer? Or as a Canadian? Certainly both of those things have shaped her profoundly, but it feels somehow diminishing to me. If I think of her in any subcategory it's in the even more limited one of great writers. Like Henry James. But that seems a more expansive, and finally more welcoming, way to consider her work: Where does she fit into what Louise Glück called the conversation with the great dead?

Which is not to say there aren't problems to be addressed. I had lunch with a gay editor regarding this memoir. He liked it, but he wanted to have a little heart-to-heart with me, one gay man to another, about the "whole gay thing." Apparently the whole gay thing was "over." Even more, the whole AIDS thing was over. I remember thinking that I knew an awful lot of people on a regimen of drugs, and that I'd heard of millions more over in Africa who couldn't even get drugs, who'd be very surprised to hear that the "whole AIDS thing was over." Besides, my book wasn't even about AIDS. John died of lung cancer.

In a way, I felt like Cynthia Ozick in her essay "We Are the Crazy Lady" when Lionel Trilling keeps mistaking her for a crazy woman in class simply because she is the only other woman there. I was gay, John was sick, and I was therefore, willy-nilly, part of the supposedly now-dead literature of AIDS. But, but . . . But nothing. The editor simply shook his head sadly and asked if I could write something that maybe had a gay character in it, but wasn't, well, so gay.

Except that I already had. Sometimes I wrote about gay people and sometimes I wrote about straight people. I didn't want anyone telling me what I should and should not be writing about. Especially not a gay person telling me to write less gay, which seemed perverse. But I also didn't want gay people telling me that I should write more gay, that my only proper subjects were gay people who should somehow be pillars of the community because there were already enough villainous stereotypes out there. I want what I write to be judged as either good or bad. These conversations have very little to do with art and everything to do with sociology or politics. And they're worthless to a writer when he's writing.

As far as I was concerned, publishing me only because I was gay was as bad as not publishing me only because I was gay. There was a time when we were expected to applaud anything that was gay simply because it was gay, and that was useful in axing down certain doors. But it always seemed to me that there was no small amount of self-condescension at work there, that we were patting our own little heads and attaching our little drawings to the fridge with magnets. I found it sort of insulting.

For me, this book is more descriptive of what you might call a post–gay sensibility. We live in a time where it is possible for our sexuality to be more integrated into our lives, and not necessarily to be the centerpiece of them. After all, we get the flu, our mothers die, our zippers catch, we walk our dogs in the park, we're on a diet. I'd be lucky to have my work considered part of the gay canon, but I also hope that it has a larger resonance than that. Doesn't every writer?

Questions and
Topics for Discussion

1. Wesley Gibson begins the memoir with his move to New York City. What kind of expectations does he have for his life there? How are these shaped by his earlier experiences as a visitor to Manhattan?

2. The transition from small towner to New Yorker is not always as smooth as Gibson had anticipated. What kind of culture shock does he come up against in his new home? How, if at all, does living in the city change him?

3. Gibson has a number of peculiar experiences either working or seeking work, from waiting tables to telemarketing, from teaching aspiring writers to interviewing until he's literally blue in the face. How is finding a vocation part of making a home for himself in the world? How does he define himself apart from his various professions?

4. When Gibson first moves into the apartment, he feels he has almost nothing in common with his roommate John. Nevertheless an unexpected bond develops between them. What kind of common ground do they find? How do Gibson's feelings about John change over the course of the book?

5. Gibson's memories of his family indicate both a deep sense of belonging (pages 92–94) and a feeling of alienation (pages 69–73). How did growing up gay in Virginia affect his ideas of family, community, and identity? How did they influence his decision to move to New York?

6. Gibson discusses the often tenuous lines of communication between gay men and straight men (page 91). Why does he say that he generally feels more at home with women

friends? In what way is his communication with other gay men in the book also muddled?

7. What role does writing and teaching writing play in Gibson's life? Why is his student Ngong's progress such a source of hope for him?

8. Death is a dominant theme in this memoir. Early on, Gibson makes light of his hypochondria, but he later loses someone close to home. How does Gibson's perception of his own mortality change? What conclusions, if any, does the book draw about the meaning of death?

9. Gibson talks about a "world where friends were family, and family were strangers" (page 231). How does the book deal with conventional notions of family? What kind of role do friends play in Gibson's life?

10. If this is a "memoir of arrival," then where does Gibson finally arrive when the book concludes?

Wesley Gibson's suggestions for further reading

Two books that were very influential to me in their use of the American vernacular were *I Lost It at the Movies* by Pauline Kael and *United States: Essays 1952–1992* by Gore Vidal. Kael's great influence was her use of the American vernacular to talk about serious critical and aesthetic issues. I think that's why she was so popular — you felt like you were engaged in a personal dialogue with her, one-on-one. I know I used to walk around arguing with her in my head. A lot of people did that. Vidal's voice, although it's astonishingly learned, is also very natural. Like Kael, he gives you that sense of someone speaking, and speaking directly to you.

A Supposedly Fun Thing I'll Never Do Again by David Foster Wallace was a book that, in the ambition of its language, for me seemed to expand the possibility of nonfiction. The language explored a vision that was overtly personal and idiosyncratic; though a lot of it is reportage, it made no pretense of objectivity. Its hilarity discovers a kind of found, dark, homegrown American surrealism that's very much rooted in what's actual. And that interests me a great deal.

One of my favorite story collections is *The Complete Stories* by Flannery O'Connor. O'Connor had a huge influence on me as a writer. I would read a paragraph of hers and then I would write a paragraph, and that's really how I learned to write.

Another favorite is *The Collected Stories of Katherine Anne Porter*. There is a novella in this collection called "Pale Horse, Pale Rider" that has an incredible description of a woman going to the brink of death and back. But I really love all of it. Porter is a wonderful writer.

I love these four novels: *Oh!* by Mary Robison, *Memento Mori* by Muriel Spark, *Breaking and Entering* by Joy Williams, and *Mrs. Dalloway* by Virginia Woolf. I know I've been more influenced by women writers than by men writers. I'm at a loss to say why, but I think it must go back to being curled up at my aunts' feet, listening to their stories.

Perhaps an odd addition to this list is *The Lord of the Rings* cycle by J. R. R. Tolkien. I've read the whole cycle at least three times: first when I was eleven, then when I was in college, and then again in my early thirties. I loved them each time. I think the first time I was just entranced by this magical world in the same way the kids are with the Harry Potter books, which I also love, though they're not nearly as dense. The second time I think I understood better how deeply imagined they really were and was sort of awed by that. And the third time, I think it was the language. It's not particularly beautiful. In fact a lot of it is little better than workmanlike. But it does have an incredible density and complexity; and then there's all the language he just created. It's extraordinary.

As I was writing *You Are Here,* I was most interested in trying to re-create an aspect of my voice on the page, and in the process describing real experience and organizing it into a narrative that actually meant something. I was certainly thinking about books such as Joan Didion's early essays, as in *Slouching Towards Bethlehem;* James Baldwin's *The Fire Next Time;* Edmund White's *States of Desire;* Quentin Crisp's *The Naked Civil Servant;* Florence King's *Confessions of a Failed Southern Lady;* and Jonathan Raban's *Old Glory: A Voyage Down the Mississippi.* I think what struck or moved me about all those books was how these authors managed to locate a highly personal voice into the larger context of things.

Jo Ann Beard's *The Boys of My Youth* was also an influence. Beard was one of the first people to use the strategies of fiction in the personal essay. You get the meaning of the essay in the same way you do when reading fiction — through narrative, the language, metaphor — instead of being told the meaning by the author as you would in a more conventional essay.

About the Author

Wesley Gibson is the author of *Shelter,* a novel, and has received fellowships from Yaddo, MacDowell, the Virginia Center for the Creative Arts, and Brown University. He has also received a New York Foundation for the Arts grant, the *Mississippi Review* Fiction Prize 2000, and the Virginia Commission for the Arts grant. He has taught writing at New York University, the University of Richmond, and Vassar College. He lives in New York City.